The Meatless Meal Guide...

for Budget-minded, Health Conscious Cooks

Tomi Ryan &
James H. Ryan, M.D.

SECOND EDITION

Fifth printing: April 1977

OTHER BOOKS BY THE AUTHORS:

The Meat Stretcher Meal Guide...
    for budget-minded, health conscious cooks
The Great Cook Writes a Book
Gourmet My Way

PUBLISHED BY:

THE RYAN COMPANY

2188 Latimer Lane, Los Angeles, Ca. 90024

This book is affectionately dedicated to

Natasha

Our love, joy and constant inspiration

Colored Text Paper:
    Wausau Paper Company's 70# Astroparche

Printed in the USA by:
    ColorGraphics Inc., Los Angeles

Bound in the USA by:
    Dependable Folding & Binding Co., Los Angeles

Graphic Art Consultant:
    Mr. Tim Bryant

CONTENTS

THE SECOND EDITION

"It is upon health, not upon ill-health that our sights should be fixed."

Roger J. Willians, NUTRITION AGAINST DISEASE

The First Edition of THE MEATLESS MEAL GUIDE emerged against a backdrop of meat boycotts and outcries against high food prices. These protests proved to be a blessing in disguise for the nutritionist. For the public's attention was at once, and dramatically, drawn to the quality of our foods and how to better cope with our diminishing health food dollars.

Now, as the Second Edition of THE MEATLESS MEAL GUIDE emerges, there looms a more ominous food crises. A crises that should shake us to an even deeper concern and re-evaluation of the foods we eat. The fact is, the world is growing hungrier, and if a global food supply disaster is to be avoided we must all do more to change our patterns of eating. In particular, we must consume less meat and hope in doing so that the beleaguered farmer can quickly adjust to the changing demand. For to raise one pound of meat it takes eight to ten pounds of grain that could otherwise be used for human consumption.

What can the individual do? Dr. Jean Mayer, Professor of Nutrition, Harvard University, says, "For a start, only one step is necessary. You can begin by giving up meat two or three times a week." To this I would add, we can also do a better job by reducing our weights and waste. The humanitarian effort of course requires no sacrifice in the palatability, cost and nutrition of our meals. Beginning tomorrow may not be soon enough however, for the hungry and starving child cannot wait. Some may question whether a cookbook is a proper forum for this message. We think so, especially when it offers the recipes with which to act.

The authors wish to express their sincere appreciation and gratitude to the many who have through their helpful suggestions, cooperation and patience made this Second Edition a book we are proud of and gratefully acknowledge the permission granted by the Art Direction Book Company to use several illustrations from the book "1000 Quaint Cuts."

INTRODUCTION

"Other men live to eat, while I eat to live."

Socrates

The building blocks for good health do not require the eating of meat each and every day. Nor is it economically feasible for most people to live on a meat-rich diet. Because of the burgeoning price of meat, the budget-wise, health-conscious homemaker is left with no alternative but to incorporate many meatless meals into her menu plans.

This movement away from high priced meat is to be encouraged, not discouraged. Besides the skyrocketing price of meat dictating a lesser use of meat in the diet, a reduction in the consumption of meat is also desirable because meats are high in cholesterol, saturated fats and calories. The high calorie, fat-rich American diet is felt to contribute substantially to the epidemic of heart attacks and obesity plaguing our nation. If we are to gain in our fight against obesity and coronary heart disease, a shift to more vegetables and foods lower in calories, cholesterol and saturated fat (such as non-fat or low-fat dairy products and soft margarines) is deemed crucial.

Unfortunately, this is not the whole story. National nutritional surveys are showing our diets are becoming less nutritious over-all, particularly in foods which supply the vitamins A and C and the minerals calcium and iron. Our job then is making our health food dollars provide all the essential nutrients needed in our daily diet by making better food choices. The key, I feel, if you are fighting a losing battle with obesity, cholesterol and nutrition, is to eat preventively. Dr. David I. Solomon says it rather succinctly. "I forsee a time when each person will realize that to survive he will have to become wiser. Each person will have to build a... flexible... philosophy... wherein he continuously eliminates, if possible, things that are wrong for him and tries to introduce what is right.

In an effort to help the homemaker come to grips with the soaring food prices, and the nutritional crises, we have put together this collection of meatless recipes. The recipes are from a file of recipes my wife, Tomi, and I have been developing for over ten years in an effort to improve and maintain our own good health. Because of the urgency of the present situation, we have decided to share them with you. In using this book, may we suggest you select a recipe that particularly intrigues you, and then plan the rest of your "meatless" meal by choosing complementary recipes from among the other courses.

It is our hope that this book will serve as a constant reminder for everyone to shop selectively among the lower priced, nutritionally wholesome foods. That is, if one wants to effectively stamp out rising food prices, and secure a foothold against obesity and heart disease. Therefore, in the words of Sir Kenelm Digby (1669), "I think it unhandsome, if not injurious, by the trouble of any further Discourse, to detain thee any longer from falling to, Fall to therefore, and much good may it do thee."

Los Angeles, California   *James H. Ryan, M.D.*

Meatless meals are not only economical, but fun, flavorful and highly nutritious.

"One swears by wholemeal bread, one by sour milk; vegetarianism is the only road to salvation of some, others insist not only on vegetables alone, but on eating those raw. At one time the only thing that matters is calories; at another time they are crazy about vitamins or about roughage.
The scientific truth may be put quite briefly; eat moderately, having an ordinary mixed diet, and don't worry."

Sir Robert Hutchinson

1. One can easily meet, or exceed, the minimum daily nutritional requirements of the average healthy person by selecting from a well-chosen, wide variety of foods. However, since foods differ so greatly in their nutritional content, we like to use a BASIC FOUR PLUS ONE system of food selection. We emphasize the familiar Basic Four Food Groups for nutritional protection and the Plus Food Group for furnishing the additional calories and fats needed in our diet for added energy and palatability. The Plus Group, which provides only insignificant amounts of nutrients, we view as the villian group in terms of obesity, excess fat and high food costs.

2. The Basic Four Food Groups, and the number of minimum recommended daily servings, consist of: the Vegetables and Fruit Group with at least 4 half cup servings; the Milk and Milk Products Group with at least 2-4 one cup servings, depending on age; the enriched Breads and Cereals Group with at least 4 servings; and the Meat Group with at least 2 servings to total 6 ounces.

3. The Plus Group consists of snack, party and dessert foods, other sweets and beverages, fats, oils, butter, margarine, salad dressings and mayonnaise, along with unenriched and refined cereals. The Plus Foods are often found mixed-in, or used as additions to, other foods. When the Plus Foods predominate you are getting "empty calories" at the expense of eating something more nutritious. We attempt to hold the Plus Food calories to less than 25 percent of our total calorie intake and let the fats from all the food groups contribute no more than a third of the calorie total.

4. The non-meat protein rich foods include dried beans, peas, nuts and peanut butter. Enriched flours, breads and cereals can contribute significant amounts of low quality protein when eaten in sufficient amounts. Although peanuts, pecans and almonds are complete proteins, these and other non-meat protein alternatives should be mixed or supplemented with a complete protein, such as cheese, milk, eggs or other dairy product, at the same meal. Canned fish should not be overlooked as a high quality source of protein and an inexpensive means of adding variety to meatless meals.

5. Build your menu plans and shopping lists around the BASIC FOUR PLUS ONE FOOD GROUPS. However, do not let the Plus Foods compete with the Basic Foods when satisfying your nutritional needs. If sacrifices must be made, budget out the Plus Foods. Therefore, to avoid nutritional deficiencies, eat from the Basic Groups and augment with the Plus Foods - the plus calorie, plus cost group.

NUTRITIONAL
GUIDELINES

OBESITY

Fat people overeat
To feed yesterday, and tomorrow.
At the end of the line, today
Never gets enough. They suffer
Not so much from gluttony
As starvation.
from SLIM PICKINGS

Taking pounds off is one thing. Keeping them off is another. When that urge to overindulge strikes, quickly turn to this section and let the following words of wisdom guide you through the crises. Then turn to the recipes to satisfy your diet requirements. Eating more meatless meals can be a helpful low-calorie solution to a nagging weight problem. Meatless meals also have the added advantage of being low in cholesterol & saturated fats.

"One must eat in measure." CARAKA SAMHITA. An ancient Hindu medical book.

"It's this damned belly that gives a man his worst troubles." Homer, ODYSSEY

"Persons who are naturally fat are apt to die earlier than those who are slender."

Hippocrates, Father of Medicine

"Anything in excess is exceedingly detrimental... particularly to the body, and it pays to reduce what is in any manner burdensome." Pliny the Elder, Roman scholar

"Excessive eating is like a deadly poison to the body of any man and it is the principle cause of all illnesses." Moses ben Maimonides, 12th century physician

"O gluttony, it is to thee we owe our griefs." Chaucer, CANTERBURY TALES

"Dyet, Health's kindest nurse." Henry Buttes, DYETS DRY DINNER, 1599

"It is a diet-book, wherein the sins of every day are written."
EPISTLE CHRISTIAN BROTHER, 1624

"In Gluttony there must be Eating, in Drunkenness there must be drinking: 'tis not the eating, nor 'tis not the drinking that is to be blamed, but the Excess." John Selden, TABLE TALK, 1654

"Mankind, since the improvement of cookery, eats twice as much as nature requires." POOR RICHARDS ALMANACK

"Persons living very entirely on vegetables are seldom of a plump and succulent habit." William Cullen, 18th century English physician

"We never repent of having eaten too little." Thomas Jefferson, 1825

"Lock up the mouth, and you have gained the victory." Sydney Smith, 1845

"The proper concept of a diet is a chicken wrung out in hot water." Martin Fisher

"Glutton, a person who escapes moderation by committing dyspepsia." THE DEVIL'S DICTIONARY

"He that eats till he is sick must fast till he is well." Old English Proverb

"A mature fat man excites pity, like a ship well stocked for its last voyage."
Ramon y Cajal, 19th century Spanish physician and anatomist

"Obeseness is the most sensitive of our aliments." George Meredith, ONE OF OUR CONQUERORS, 1891

"Imprisoned in every fat man a thin man is wildly signalling to be let out." Cyril Connolly

"If you wish to grow thinner, diminish your dinner." A time honored remedy.

"In eating, a third of the stomach should be filled with food, a third with drink, and the rest left empty."
A medical aphorism.

"The food you eat today you wear tomorrow." An old saying.

"Spare tires belong on cars, not on people." Lifestyle Programs, Inc.

"Overeating is one of the greatest hazzards to life in our country today." W. David Steed, M.D.

"Aside from the shameless artistic error involved in exhibiting a monstrous figure, the heart of the rotund has enough to do in irrigating some hundred-weight of adipose tissue."
Ramon y Cajal, M.D.

"Middle-aged men who are 20 per cent overweight have about three times the risk of a fatal heart attack compared with middle-aged men of normal weight."
American Heart Association

FATSVILLE AND THINSVILLE

There once was a young maiden from Thinsville
Who beguiled the eyes of King Fatsville.
He took up her chase with haste
But soon was out paced and disgraced
When a coronary put him in Docsville.

King Fatsville recovered with haste and again gave chase
While keeping pace with nitroglycerine by the case.
The fleet-footed young maiden fair
Became Queen with health as her flair.
And now his grace, finds less calories and cholesterol commonplace.

Dr. Jim

THE RECIPES

FEASTING

"Here's to your health and your family's good health. May you live long and prosper."

Joseph Jefferson,
RIP VAN WINKLE

"And here's to the housewife that's thrifty."

R.B. Sheridan,
SCHOOL FOR SCANDAL

We encourage you to alter the recipes to satisfy your own taste preferences
and to substitute with ingredients on hand.

TIPS ON USING THE BOOK

1. Uncomplicating menu planning has been a long sought after goal. We hope to have taken some of the fidget and scramble out by color coding the various courses, appetizers through desserts. A complete meal can be put together with quickness and ease by simply referring to the various colored sections. Or you can select a recipe that particularly intrigues you, and then plan the rest of your meal by choosing complementary recipes from among the other recipe sections.

2. You need not restrict yourself to using these recipes only in meatless meals. The recipes are highly versatile and many may be used in entertaining. You may also find some recipes listed in one course, useful in a different course.

3. The task, and often drudgery, of following some recipe formats is too often more than one can bear. You will be able to make short work of checking the ingredients and following the directions with our open, straightforward format. A glance will usually be sufficient. If you don't have all the ingredients, please substitute. Some of the great things about meatless meals are their adaptability, speed and the success with which you can change the recipes.

4. Use this book as a workbook in developing your own meatless recipes. Improvise and create your own exciting ideas by writing the changes right on the recipe pages.

5. For convenience, stocking frozen and canned items is helpful. However, we prefer fresh ingredients when they are of high quality, low price and in-season.

6. Keep the cooking times of all vegetables short and the amount of cooking water to a minimum. By doing so more nutrients are retained and flavors, colors and textures preserved.

INTERCHANGEABLES

A useful guide for determining the equivalent in cups of either the fresh, canned or frozen vegetable. A rule-of-thumb is to equate one 10-ounce package of frozen vegetable, or one 16-ounce can, to about 2 cups or 3 servings.

	1-POUND FRESH	CUPS, CUT	CAN SIZE	FROZEN PKG.
Asparagus	16-20 med. stalks	2 cups	16-ounce	10-ounce
Beets	3-4 medium	2 cups	16-ounce	
Broccoli	1 medium	2 cups		10-ounce
Brussels Sprouts	13-15	2 cups		10-ounce
Cabbage	1/2 sm. head	4 cups		
Carrots	7-8 medium	2 1/2 cups	16-ounce	16-ounce
Cauliflower	1 med. head	2 cups		10-ounce
Celery	1 med. bunch	2 1/2 cups		
Corn	4 ears	1 1/2 cups	12-ounce	10-ounce
Eggplant	1 medium	2 1/2 cups		
Green Beans	50 large	3 cups	16-ounce	2 9-ounce
Lima Beans	2 1/2 c. dried	6 c. cooked	6-8 ounce	4 10-ounce
Mushrooms	35-40 med.	5 cups	4-8 ounce	2 6-ounce
Peas	1-lb. shelled	1 cup	8-ounce	10-ounce
Onions	3-4 medium	2 1/2 cups	16-ounce	12-ounce
Potatoes	3 medium	2 1/2 cups	16-ounce	10-ounce
Spinach	2 bunches	1 1/2 cups	15-ounce	10-ounce
Summer Squash	1 pound	2 cups	16-ounce	10-ounce
Zucchini	3 medium	2 cups		10-ounce
Winter Squash	1 pound	2 cups		12-ounce
Sweet Potatoes	2 medium	2 1/2 cups	16-ounce	
Tomatoes	3 medium	2 cups	16-ounce	

ABBREVIATIONS

c.	= cup	oz.	= ounce
cond.	= condensed	opt.	= optional
env.	= envelope	pd.	= powder
fr.	= frozen	pkg.	= package
grad.	= gradually	qt.	= quart
hr.	= hour	refrig.	= refrigerate
ingred.	= ingredients	sm.	= small
lb.	= pound	t.	= teaspoon
lg.	= large	T.	= tablespoon
med.	= medium	temp.	= temperature
min.	= minutes	veg.	= vegetable

CHEESY BANANA

1 lg. whole banana
1 t. lemon juice

} rub banana with juice

creamy sharp cheddar cheese

} completely coat banana with cheese

chopped nuts (black walnuts if
available)

} roll in nuts and place on plate garnished
with greenery

to serve: slice off portions and serve with
picks or on a cracker

serves: 4

TIPSY EDAM

1 7-oz. Edam cheese round

} slice circle from top of round
scoop out cheese leaving ⅛ inch thick wall

¼ lb. soft margarine

} add margarine to cheese
blend until smooth

¼ c. beer
2 T. brandy
1 T. grated onion

} mix in these 3 ingred.
pile finished blend into shell
chill

parsley

} garnish

crackers

} serve at room temp. with crackers

serves: 14-16

ORANGE-TWIST TUNA COCKTAIL

1 7-oz. can tuna, drained
2 c. orange sections
3 T. sliced green onions   } combine these 6 ingredients
2 T. orange juice   cover
¼ t. salt   chill
dash pepper

¼ c. chopped pecans   } when ready to serve
¼ c. chopped ripe olives   stir in these 2 ingred.

6 lettuce cups   } pile in lettuce cups or in lettuce lined cocktail
                    glasses

dallop of mayonnaise or   } top with your choice
sour cream

serves: 6

JAPANESE PIN WHEELS

8 hard cooked egg whites
½ t. salt   } mash together these 3 ingred.
½ t. sugar

4 hard-cooked egg yolks
¼ t. salt   } mash together these 3 ingred.
dash sugar

Pat egg white mixture on a wet 5x8 inch cloth
Press egg yolk mixture evenly over top of whites
leaving a 1 inch margin at ends and sides
Holding one end of cloth   peel off while rolling up
jelly roll fashion
Wrap roll in the cloth tying ends securely
Lay on rack in pan with shallow amount of boiling
water
Steam covered 8-10 min.
Remove from pan
Chill
to serve: unwrap and slice 24 slices

MISS SWISS

½ lb. Swiss cheese
½ onion
} finely grate these 2 ingred.

dash salt
dash pepper
} add these 2 ingred.

cocktail crackers
} spread mixture on top of crackers

margarine
} dot with margarine

broil to melt cheese

serve hot

serves: 8

DOLMA

½ c. olive oil
5 c. chopped onions

} gently saute onions until golden

1 c. rice
2 T. salt
1 c. water

} add these 3 ingred.
cover
cook 20 min.

½ c. raisins
½ c. pine nuts
½ c. tomato sauce
¼ c. water
½ t. allspice
½ t. cinnamon
dash pepper

} add these 7 ingred.
cover
cook 4 min.

1 head cabbage

(continued next page)

} immerse cabbage in boiling water a few
min. to soften outer leaves
remove softened leaves
place 1 T. filling on each leaf
roll leaves to enclose filling

(DOLMA continued)

1 sliced onion
} place onion on bottom of baking dish
place rolls, seams down, side by side on onion

water
} add water to cover

bake at 350° 1 hr.

serve at room temp. or cold
may eat with fingers

SIZZLING OLIVES

7 oz. can pitted, ripe olives
1 lg. clove garlic, minced
} combine undrained olives and garlic for at least 4 days

2 T. olive oil
} heat oil in pan
add drained olives
heat gently 1 min.

serves: 6

PARMESAN DIPS

5 T. margarine

} melt margarine in pan

1/3 c. flour
1/3 c. cornstarch

} mix in these 2 ingred.

1½ c. milk

} grad. stir in milk
cook 5 min. stirring

7 T. Parmesan cheese
¼ t. chili pd.
½ t. salt
dash pepper

} add these 4 ingred.
cook 2 min.
remove from heat

2 eggs, well beaten

} grad. beat in eggs
cover with wax paper
chill at least 2 hrs.
cut into 1 inch cubes

flour
beaten egg
bread crumbs

} coat with each of these 3 ingred. in the order given

"MILK BELOW, MAIDS!"

(continued next page)

deep fat 400°   } fry until golden - about 1½ min.
                                       drain

1 c. tomato sauce   } combine these 2 ingred.
1 T. horseradish   use as dip

                                       serves: 6-8

ONION TANGS

3 T. minced onion
3 T. mayonnaise
dash salt   } combine these 5 ingred.
dash pepper
dash tabasco sauce

10 to 12 cocktail crackers   } spread mixture on crackers
                                       broil 5 min.   serve hot

TAPENADE STUFFED CELERY

½ c. chopped black olives
10 anchovies with capers
7 oz. can tuna
1/3 c. chopped parsley
3 T. brandy
1 t. dry mustard
1½ c. mayonnaise

blend these 7 ingred. until smooth

2 inch lengths of celery

stuff celery (or use as vegetable dip)

makes 3 cups

CONFETTI DIP

1 lg. firm tomato, chopped
1 T. instant bell pepper flakes
¼ c. lemon juice
½ t. salt
¼ t. pepper
dash garlic salt
dash celery salt
½ t. worcestershire sauce

combine these 8 ingred.
marinate 1 hr.

¼ c. minced green onions
2 c. sour cream

mix in these 2 ingred.
serve as dip for vegetables

makes 3 cups

CHILI NUTS

1 lb. shelled almonds or peanuts
1 T. chili pd.
dash cumin
1 clove garlic, mashed
¼ c. margarine
} combine these 5 ingred. in pan
saute stirring until light brown
remove garlic

salt } sprinkle with salt

serve hot or cool
store in jars

PROUD PUFFS

¼ c. soft margarine
6 oz. soft sharp cheese
½ c. flour
dash cayenne
dash chili pd.
} combine these 5 ingred. until smooth
chill 1 hr.
roll into walnut size balls
(may be stored in refrigerator or freezer at this point)

bake at 350° 10 min. serves: 4-6

TUNA PATE

6 oz. cream cheese
2 T. catsup
3 T. minced parsley
¼ c. minced onion
¾ T. worcestershire sauce
¼ t. tabasco sauce
2 7-oz. cans tuna, drained

} blend these 7 ingred. until smooth

¾ c. sliced ripe olives
¼ c. chopped pecans

} stir in these 2 ingred.
chill

wonderful served as dip or filling for vegetables and crackers

makes 3½ cups

WHEATS CURRIED

1/3 c. margarine
½ t. curry pd.
¼ t. onion salt
⅛ t. ginger

} combine these 4 ingred. in pan
heat to melt

2½ c. spoon-sized Shredded
Wheat biscuits

} toss in wheats to coat

heat gently 5 min. stirring

serve warm

serves: 4

CRACKER PUFFS

saltine crackers } soak saltines in water 5 min.
with slotted spatula carefully place on
greased cooky sheet

melted margarine } brush with margarine

bake 350° 20-25 min. until light and crisp

grated sharp cheese
chili pd. or cumin } sprinkle top with these 3 ingred.
paprika

return to oven to melt cheese

serve hot

MOCK LIVER PATE

3 T. margarine
½ c. chopped scallions
1½ lb. mushrooms, sliced

combine these 3 ingred. in pan
saute 10 min

2 hard-boiled eggs
2 T. cond. milk
1½ t. salt
¼ t. white pepper
dash worcestershire sauce

add these 5 ingred.
blend until smooth paste
chill

serves: 6

SPLIT PEA SOUP

2 qts. water
2 c. split peas
4 stalks celery, chopped
2 carrots, chopped
1 onion, chopped
¼ t. thyme
dash cayenne
1 bay leaf
½ t. minced parsley
¼ t. garlic salt
1½ t. salt
pepper

combine these 12 ingred.

bring to boil

simmer until peas are tender

puree smooth

serves: 8

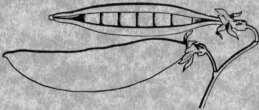

VEGETABLE HEALTH SOUP

1 c. Red Cereal Wheat or
    other whole grain cereal
4 c. water
2 bouillon cubes

combine these 3 ingred.
soak 3 hrs.

1 bunch carrots
4 stalks celery
1 bunch green onions with tops
1 T. salt
½ t. oregano
½ t. basil

chop vegetables
add these 6 ingred.
simmer 2 hrs.

1 lb. green beans, sliced

add beans

simmer 15 min.

serves: 6

QUICKIE BEAN SOUP

1 can beef consomme
1 can black bean soup
1½ cans water

} combine these 3 ingred.
heat well

dash vermouth

} add if desired

croutons
sieved egg yolk

} garnish to serve

serves: 4-6

VEGETARIAN SOUP

3 c. cooked wheat or barley
6 carrots, scrape and slice
4 stalks celery with tops, chopped
1 head cauliflower, break apart
6 leaves Swiss chard or
  spinach, chopped
1 can corn, drained
2 lg. cans stewed tomatoes
3 t. parsley
1½ T. instant minced onion
1½ T. instant minced peppers
2 t. chervil
3 T. salt

combine all ingred.
cover
simmer ½ hr.

serves: 6

"Avena", Oats [Mattioli, *Commentarii*, 1560]

COLD APPLE SOUP

1 lb. cooking apples, chopped 4½ c. water ½ T. grated lemon peel 1 inch stick cinnamon pinch salt ¼ c. sugar	combine these 6 ingred. cover cook until apples are tender remove cinnamon puree return to pan
1 T. cornstarch ½ T. cold water	combine these 2 ingred. add to soup cook stirring until thickened
1 T. lemon juice ¼ c. white wine	stir in these 2 ingred.
sour cream	serve with dallop of sour cream

serves: 4

LENTIL SOUP

½ lb. lentils } cover lentils with water
soak 4 hrs.
drain

5 c. water
3 carrots, sliced
2 onions, sliced
1 slice of unpeeled orange
few drops tabasco sauce
1 T. minced parsley   add these 11 ingred.
1 bay leaf   cover
5 peppercorns   simmer 1 to 1½ hrs.
1 lg. clove garlic, minced   remove orange and bay leaf
1 t. celery salt
3 t. salt

¼ c. sherry } add if desired

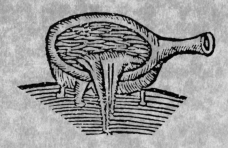

serves: 6-8

PLUM SWIZZLE

1¼ lb. ripe plums, chopped } combine these 5 ingred.
½ c. water   cover
¼ c. sugar   cook 20 min.
1 inch piece cinnamon stick   remove cinnamon and cloves
2 whole cloves   puree smooth

1 c. sour cream } blend in sour cream
                   chill well

sour cream   } serve with a dollop of sour cream
cinnamon   sprinkle with cinnamon

serves: 6

TROPIC BISQUE

4-5 ripe bananas
3 c. milk
¾ c. sour cream

} blend these 3 ingred. until smooth
chill

3 slices white bread
½ c. soft margarine

} spread margarine on bread
cut into croutons
place on baking sheet
bake at 400° until bread is toasted lightly

3 T. cinnamon sugar

} sprinkle over croutons
return to oven to melt slightly

serve croutons with soup

serves: 4

SOPA DE AJO BLANCO

2 slices bread, cubed
2 T. olive oil
10 blanched almonds
3 cloves garlic, mashed

} combine these 4 ingred.
saute until bread is golden
mash to a paste

3 c. chicken broth
1 t. salt
dash pepper

} mix in these 3 ingred.
chill well

to serve

1 c. cubed melon or
    seeded grapes
6 ice cubes

} stir in fruit
place ice cube in each bowl
top with soup

serves: 6

CARROT BISQUE

3 c. peeled sliced carrots
2 c. water
dash salt

} combine these 3 ingred.
cook 25 min.

2 chicken bouillon cubes
½ c. sour cream
½ t. sugar

} add these 3 ingred.
puree smooth in blender

croutons

} serve with croutons

serves: 4

ARTICHOKE SOUP

1 pkg. frozen artichoke hearts
pinch Fines Herbes
2 cans chicken broth
¼ t. salt
pepper

} combine these 5 ingred.
cook 5 min.
puree

1 c. light cream

} add cream   gently reheat

parsley

} garnish

serve hot or cold

serves: 4

1 c. minced onion
2½ c. diced potatoes
2 leeks, diced
4 T. margarine

combine these 4 ingred.
saute 15 min.

4 c. bouillon
¼ c. chopped parsley
pinch chervil
pinch sage
salt to taste
¼ t. pepper

add these 6 ingred.
cover
simmer ½ hr.

2 bunches spinach

add spinach

cook 5 min.
puree smooth

1 pkg. frozen peas

add peas

heat to serving temp. only   serves: 6

EMERALD SOUP

1 can cond. asparagus soup
1¼ c. milk
1 T. instant minced onion
½ t. instant garlic
dash nutmeg
6 egg yolks
salt to taste
dash pepper

} combine these 8 ingred.

1 pkg. frozen peas, thawed

} divide peas into 6 buttered oven proof
soup bowls or cups
top with soup

bake 350° for ½ hr.
top will be partially set

serves: 6

SHORT-CUT SPINACH SOUP

1 can cond. potato soup
1 can water
1 pkg. frozen or 2 c. chopped spinach
} combine these 3 ingred.
cook 10 min.

4 T. dry sherry
1 T. instant minced onion
salt to taste
dash pepper
} add these 4 ingred.

mace } lightly sprinkle with mace to serve

serves: 4

PEPPER SOUP POT

12 green and red bell peppers
6 onions
½ bunch celery
3 tomatoes

} chop these 4 vegetables

2 c. quick cooking rice

} add rice
add water to reach to top of vegetables

½ t. basil
½ t. summer savory
½ t. crumbled bay leaf
¼ t. cumin
¼ t. coriander
2 T. salt

} add herbs to your liking and availability
cover
bring to boil
simmer 5 min.

serves: 8

VEGETARIAN DELIGHT

2 dozen ripe tomatoes	scald in boiling salted water 1 min. peel core mash
4 lg. onions, chopped 1 clove garlic, mashed 1 T. vegetable oil	combine these 3 ingred. in pan saute 5 min.
7 stalks celery 6 green peppers 5 lg. carrots 1 bunch parsley	chop these 4 vegetables combine with onions and tomatoes
4 c. bouillon or more if desired 1 T. salt ¼ t. pepper 2 bay leaves	add liquid and seasoning simmer 15 min.

1 pkg. lime jello	} prepare jello as pkg. directs

2 T. mayonnaise
1 c. chopped celery
½ t. minced onion
1 T. lemon juice
1 c. diced avocado
¼ t. salt

} when jello is almost set fold in these 6 ingred.

½ c. cream

} whip cream
fold in

pour into mold
chill until set

serves: 4

CHERRY FRUIT SALAD

2 heads butter or red lettuce   } line 6 salad bowls with leaves
shred remaining lettuce

1 cantaloupe, cubed
2 c. pineapple chunks, drained
1 avocado, diced
1 lg. can Royal Ann
   or Bing Cherries   } add these 6 ingred. to lettuce
½ t. salt   chill ½ hr.
juice of ½ lemon

serves: 6

water cress } line salad bowls with cress

toast } place toast on top

cranberry sauce, 2 slices } top with 2 slices cranberry sauce

crabmeat
mayonnaise } combine these 4 ingred.
salt to taste mound on top of cranberry sauce
squeeze lemon juice

KIDNEY BEAN SALAD

1 lg. can kidney beans, drained
1 stalk celery, diced
1 lg. onion, chopped
4 T. pickle relish
} combine these 4 ingred.

½ c. white wine vinegar
½ c. sugar
1 egg, beaten
2 t. dry mustard
} combine these 4 ingred.
bring to a boil
pour over beans
refrigerate at least 6 hrs.

chill until ready to serve

serves: 4

CEASAR SALAD

1 head romaine lettuce   }   cut lettuce into bite-size pieces

½ t. dry mustard
¼ t. garlic salt
¼ t. pepper
½ t. salt
¼ c. Parmesan cheese
6 T. olive oil
3 T. wine vinegar

} add these 7 ingred. to lettuce
vary according to taste
toss well

2 eggs

} boil eggs 1 min.
break eggs into lettuce
toss well

croutons   add croutons and toss

serves: 4

ORANGE YOGHURT SALAD

2 oranges, peel and section
4 T. instant minced toasted onions
1 c. yoghurt
2 t. sugar

} combine these 4 ingred.

lettuce

} serve on bed of lettuce

serves: 4

FRUIT TREAT

orange sections
cantaloupe balls
peach slices
apricot halves
miniature marshmallows (opt.)

1 c. yoghurt

} combine these 6 ingred.
serve well chilled or frozen on bed of
lettuce

V-8 MOLD

1 pkg. unflavored gelatin } sprinkle gelatin over juice
½ c. cold V-8 juice   } stand 5 min. to soften

1 c. hot V-8 juice   } stir in juices
½ t. lemon juice   } chill until partially set

½ c. cooked corn   } stir in these 4 ingred.
½ c. radishes, sliced   } mold
½ c. celery, sliced   } chill until firm
6 green onions, chopped   }

cottage cheese   } garnish with cottage cheese

serves: 4

CRIMSON CANDLES

1 lb. can whole cranberry sauce } heat cranberries to dissolve

3 oz. strawberry jello
½ c. boiling water } dissolve jello in water

1 T. lemon juice
¼ t. salt } add these 2 ingred. and cranberries to jello
chill until slightly thickened

½ c. mayonnaise } add mayonnaise
beat until fluffy

1 apple, diced
¼ c. chopped walnuts } fold in these 2 ingred.
fill cranberry can ¾ full for largest can
spoon remaining jello in other assorted
smaller cans

chill firm
unmold on garnished platter

birthday candles } insert candle into each jello candle
light when served

1 lg. bunch spinach   }   tear into bite-size pieces

½ c. vinegar and oil dressing
½ c. pine nuts   }   combine these 4 ingred.
½ c. raisins   toss with spinach
½ c. chopped green onion

serves: 4-6

CURRIED TOMATO SALAD

4 tomatoes, cut in wedges
2 stalks celery, chopped
1 onion, sliced
salt

} combine these 4 ingred.
   divide onto 4 lettuce lined bowls

4 T. mayonnaise
1 t. curry pd.
2 T. minced parsley
dash salt

} combine these 4 ingred.
   divide on top of each salad

serves: 4

THE IRISHMAN AND THE SALAD OIL.

SWINGING SLAW

1 lg. ripe banana
½ c. Thousand Island Dressing   } 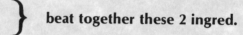 beat together these 2 ingred.

1 head cabbage, shred finely   } toss with dressing

serves: 6

ITALIAN SALAD

3 zucchini, sliced
1 red onion, slice into rings
¼ lb. mushrooms, slice
} combine these 3 ingred.

Italian Dressing
½ t. Salad Herbs
} add these 2 ingred.
toss well

serve cold

serves: 6

TANGY KUKE SALAD

½ c. sour cream
1½ T. prepared horseradish   } combine these 3 ingred.
¼ t. salt

4 cucumbers, sliced   } toss cucumbers with dressing to serve

paprika   } serve on a bed of lettuce
parsley   } garnish with these 2 ingred.

serves: 6

"FINE LARGE CUCUMBERS!"

AFRICAN HARVEST SALAD

2 oranges
2 onions
¾ c. pitted black olives

} thinly slice these 3 ingred.

2 T. olive oil
¼ t. salt
¼ t. sugar

} combine these 3 ingred.
toss with salad

serve on bed of lettuce

serves: 4

ROQUEFORT DRESSING

¼ lb. Roquefort cheese, crumble
4 T. plain yoghurt
4 T. olive oil   } combine these 6 ingred.
3 T. lemon juice   mix to blend well
salt to taste
¼ t. paprika

salad makings   } toss with salad dressing

ZUCCHINI-ONION SAUTE

1 lb. zucchini, sliced
1 onion, sliced
3 T. margarine

} combine these 3 ingred.
saute 4 min.

¼ c. vermouth (dry)

} add vermouth
simmer uncovered 1 min.

½ c. sour cream
¼ c. blanched almonds

} to serve: stir in these 2 ingred.

serves: 4

DEVILISH EGGS

6 hard-boiled eggs   } cut eggs in half lengthwise

¼ c. mayonnaise
½ t. salt
dash pepper   combine these 7 ingred. with the yolks
2 t. prepared mustard   mash well
1 T. minced celery   stuff whites
1 T. minced stuffed green olives
1 T. minced green onions

serves: 6

PAPRIKA NOODLES

1 pkg. egg noodles (6 oz.) } cook noodles as pkg. directs
drain

3 T. margarine
3 t. paprika } toss in these 3 ingred.
¼ t. seasoned salt

serves: 8

Saying Grace.

CHEESE ALMOND RICE

6 oz. sliced mushrooms, drain
2 t. instant minced onions
2 t. instant minced green peppers
1/3 c. chopped almonds
1¼ c. long grain rice
½ t. salt
dash pepper

} combine these 7 ingred. in a casserole

3½ c. water
3 bouillon cubes
4 T. soy sauce

} combine these 3 ingred.
pour over casserole

¾ c. shredded cheddar cheese

} top with cheese
bake covered 350° 45 min.

serves: 4

CHINESE RICE

¾ c. celery, chopped
½ c. mushrooms, sliced
½ c. green pepper, chopped
½ c. green onion, chopped
4 T. margarine

} combine these 5 ingred.
saute 6 min.

4 c. cooked rice
1 t. salt
dash pepper

} stir in these 3 ingred.
heat to serving temp.

2/3 c. chopped peanuts

} stir in nuts

serve with soy sauce

serves: 4

SAFFRON RICE

½ onion, minced
4 T. margarine

} saute onion until golden

1 c. rice

} add rice

small pinch pd. saffron
2 c. water
3 bouillon cubes
¼ t. salt

} combine these 4 ingred.
let bouillon dissolve
add to rice
cook covered 20 min.

let stand covered 10 min.

serves: 6

Saffron-plant (⅓ natural size).

1 onion, chopped
1 stalk celery, chopped   } saute until onion turns golden
4 t. margarine

1 c. rice   } add rice
                                   stir to coat well

2½ c. water
½ t. tumeric   } add these 4 ingred.
½ t. salt   cook covered 20 min.
dash pepper

2 T. chopped pimiento   } add these 2 ingred.
1 pkg. frozen peas   heat only to defrost peas
                                   let stand covered 5 min.

serves: 4

CRACKED WHEAT PILAF

2 T. margarine
1 c. cracked wheat
½ onion, minced

} combine these 3 ingred.

2 c. water
4 veg. bouillon cubes, dissolve
¼ t. oregano
½ t. salt
dash pepper

} add these 5 ingred.
cook covered 25 min.

serves: 4

DELUXE RICE

2 c. rice
4 c. water
1 t. salt
5 veg. bouillon cubes

} combine these 4 ingred.
cook covered 20 min.
let stand covered for 10 min.

1 onion, minced
1 clove garlic, mashed
¼ c. margarine

} combine these 3 ingred.
saute 8 min.

2/3 c. pine nuts

} roast in oven until coffee brown
add to onions

½ t. nutmeg
2 t. tumeric
¼ c. raisins plumped in sherry

} add these 3 ingred.
add rice
toss

serves: 6

CAULIFLOWER PUCKER-UP

1 head cauliflower
}
break into flowerettes
cook 5 min.
drain

1 T. olive oil
4 T. salad vinegar
½ t. salt
}
combine these 3 ingred.
cover
heat 1 min.

½ c. grated American cheese
}
sprinkle cheese over top

serves: 4

EGGPLANT FRIES

1 c. pancake mix
2 T. canned grated American
    cheese
¼ t. seasoned salt
½ c. milk

} combine these 4 ingred. to make batter

1 eggplant

} cut into ½ inch thick strips
dip into batter

2" deep veg. oil 375°

} fry a few at a time until golden
drain on absorbent paper

¾ c. tomato catsup
2 T. prepared horseradish

} combine these 3 ingred.
use as dip for eggplant

serves: 4

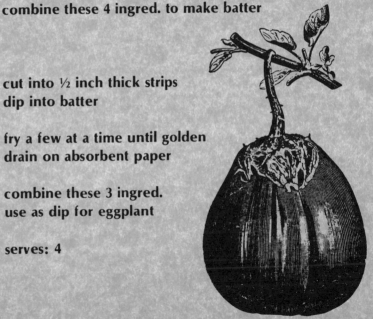

NUTTY CELERY

3 c. celery, sliced
1 onion, sliced
3 T. olive oil

} combine these 3 ingred.
saute 7 min.

¼ c. peanut butter

} stir in to melt

serves: 4

6 cooked potatoes.
½ - ¾ c. milk
¼ c. margarine
2 t. salt

} whip together these 4 ingred.

½ c. grated cheddar cheese
½ t. white pepper
¼ t. dill weed
1 pkg. chopped spinach, thawed

} stir in these 4 ingred.
bake 350° ½ hr.

serves: 8

SPANISH GREEN BEANS

2 lb. green beans } blanch in boiling salted water 5 min.
drain

1 T. vegetable oil } combine these 2 ingred.
1 onion, diced saute 5 min.

1 c. tomato catsup
½ t. chili pd. } add these 4 ingred.
½ t. salt add beans
¼ t. allspice

¼ c. grated Parmesan cheese } top with cheese

serves: 6

MOORISH SPINACH

3 lb. fresh spinach, cleaned,
    chopped
1 c. raisins
½ c. pine nuts
2 T. margarine
½ t. salt
dash pepper

}

combine these 6 ingred. in pan
cook 5 min. stirring occassionally

serves: 4-6

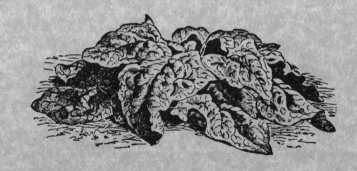

BRUSSELS SPICED

2 lbs. Brussels sprouts } blanch brussels in boiling salted water 5 min. drain

2 T. margarine
2 T. flour
1 bouillon cube } combine these 3 ingred. in pan
cook until smooth

1 c. water } gradually stir in water
cook until thickened

⅛ t. cloves
⅛ t. nutmeg
⅛ t. mace
½ t. salt } add these 4 ingred.

serves: 4-6

SAFFRON BRUSSELS

2 lbs. Brussels sprouts   } blanch brussels in boiling water 5 min.
                              drain

1 c. water
1 vegetable bouillon cube
2 T. instant wondra flour
¼ t. cloves
¼ t. nutmeg   } combine these 7 ingred. in pan
⅛ t. saffron   cook stirring until thickened and smooth
½ t. salt   pour over brussels

serves: 6

CARROTS DILLY

2 bunches carrots

} cook until crisp-tender
drain

1 c. white wine vinegar
2 t. salt
grinding pepper
1 t. dill weed
1 T. chervil

} combine these 5 ingred.
pour over carrots
cover
refrigerate 2 days or longer

serves: 6

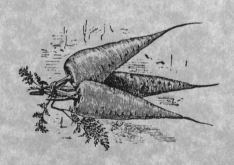

4 lg. tomatoes

} cut tomatoes in halves
place in baking dish

3 T. melted margarine
¾ t. seasoned salt
1¼ t. garlic pd.
1½ t. pd. coriander
1½ t. cumin
1 T. sesame seeds
½ c. dry bread crumbs

} combine these 7 ingred.
place on top of tomatoes
bake uncovered 300° ½ hr. or until tops
are golden brown

serves: 8

TRADITIONAL BEANS

1½ lbs. green beans } blanch in boiling salted water 5 min.
drain

2 T. margarine
¼ c. blanched almonds } saute almonds until golden

2 T. chopped parsley
1 T. prepared mustard
1 t. salt } add these 3 ingred.
mix with beans

lemon slices } serve garnished with lemon

serves: 4

6 potatoes

} cook potatoes until tender

1 c. warm milk
2 T. margarine
2 t. salt

} add these 3 ingred.
beat until fluffy

3 stalks celery, minced
1 onion, minced
1 T. vegetable oil

} combine these 3 ingred.
saute until soft - not brown

¾ c. white bread crumbs
1 T. chopped parsley
1 egg, well beaten

} add these 3 ingred.
combine with potatoes in buttered casserole
bake 350° 10 min.

¼ c. Parmesan cheese
sprinkling paprika

} top casserole with these 2 ingred.
return to oven 5 min.

serves: 6

SAUCY ZUCCHINI

4 zucchini or summer squash,
   sliced
3 T. margarine
½ t. salt

combine these 3 ingred in pan
saute stirring 5 min.

¼ c. milk
1/3 c. mayonnaise
2/3 c. grated sharp cheddar
   cheese
¼ t. salt
dash pepper

add these 5 ingred.
cook gently until cheese is melted

serves: 6

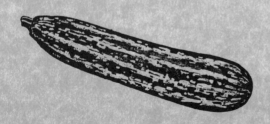

CHEEZED CHIPS

potato chips } spread chips out on baking sheet

Kraft grated American cheese } generously sprinkle with cheese
bake 300° 5-10 min.
until cheese melts

serve hot

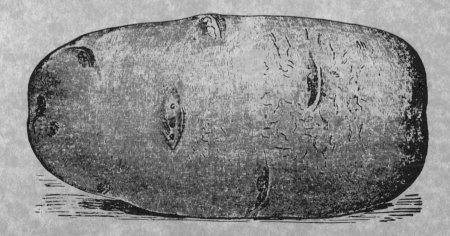

PEAS DELUXE

1 pkg. frozen peas, thawed
¼ c. mayonnaise
¼ c. sour cream
½ t. dill weed
½ t. grated lemon rind
¼ t. salt

combine these 6 ingred.
heat to serving temp. only

serves: 4

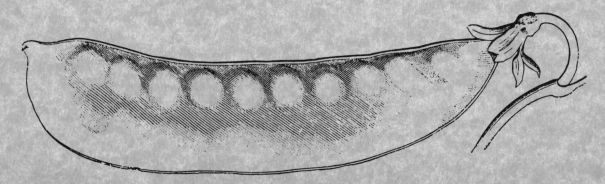

BEGEDEL DJAGUNG

1 c. uncooked corn
3 T. minced onion
½ clove garlic, minced
4 T. minced celery
2 T. minced pimientos
½ t. salt
grinding pepper
1 egg beaten
2 T. flour

combine all ingred.
pour into greased fry pan to make one
large pancake
brown on both sides
cut into wedges to serve

serves: 4

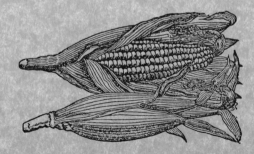

ASPARAGUS HOLLANDAISE

2 pkgs. frozen asparagus, thaw
1 can (¾ c.) hollandaise sauce
1 T. prepared mustard
1 c. green grapes, halved

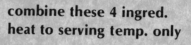

combine these 4 ingred.
heat to serving temp. only

serves: 4

ASPARAGUS ROYAL

2 pkgs. frozen asparagus ⎫
⎬ cook asparagus as pkg. directs
⎭ drain

¾ t. salt ⎫
¼ c. good chutney ⎬ stir in these 3 ingred.
¾ c. sour cream ⎭

serve hot or cold

serves: 6

GOURMET BROCCOLI

1 pkg. frozen broccoli, thawed
1 can (¾ c.) hollandaise sauce
¾ c. good chutney
¼ t. salt

combine these 4 ingred.
heat to serving temp. only

serves: 4

CORN BEIGNETS

1 c. water
¾ t. salt
½ t. sugar
¼ c. margarine

} combine these 4 ingred. in pan
bring to a boil

1 c. flour
dash nutmeg

} add these 2 ingred. all at once
stir until smooth and dough parts from
sides of pan
remove from heat

4 eggs

} beat eggs one at a time into batter

1 c. corn

} stir in corn

deep fat 380°

} drop batter into fat by tablespoon
fry until puffed & browned on both sides
drain on absorbent paper

CORN CURRY

2 c. corn, canned or frozen
2 T. instant minced onion
¼ to ½ t. curry pd.

} combine these 3 ingred.
heat to serving temp.

½ c. sour cream
½ t. salt
dash pepper

} stir in these 3 ingred.

serves: 4

EGG IN YOUR BEANS

2 lbs. green beans

} blanch beans in boiling salted water 5 min. drain

3 T. instant wondra flour
2 c. milk
2 t. dill weed
½ t. salt
2 egg yolks

} combine these 5 ingred.
cook stirring until thickened and smooth

1 t. lemon juice

} add juice and beans

serves: 6

PARMESAN FRIES

1 bag frozen french fries } prepare fries as pkg. directs

1 c. Parmesan cheese } sprinkle these 2 ingred. over hot fries
½ t. salt heat to slightly melt cheese

serve immediately

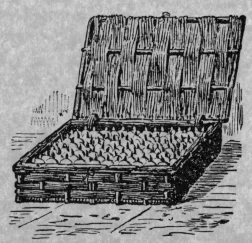

Walnut-leaved Kidney Potatoes sprouted in basket.

CHEESE CORN BREAD

2 eggs
1 c. drained corn
1 c. sour cream
¼ c. soft margarine
1 T. baking pd.
1 t. salt
1 c. cornmeal

} combine these 7 ingred.
mix well
pour ½ batter into greased 9x9 inch
cake pan

½ of 4 oz. can seeded, chopped
    green chilies
1 T. instant minced onion
½ c. grated sharp cheddar cheese

} layer these 3 ingred. over top
top with remaining batter

½ c. grated Monterey Jack cheese
paprika

} sprinkle these 2 ingred. over top
bake 350° 20-25 min.

DOUBLE CHEESE PEAS

1 pkg. frozen peas, thawed
½ t. seasoned salt

} combine these 2 ingred. in pan
heat to serving temp.

3 oz. cream cheese
½ c. cottage cheese

} combine these 2 ingred.
beat until smooth
add to peas
heat gently

serves: 4

BEANS-MUSHROOMS MADEIRA

1½ lbs. green beans } blanch beans in boiling salted water 5 min.
drain

¾ t. anise seed
2 T. margarine } combine these 4 ingred.
1 T. chopped green onions saute 5 min.
1 lb. mushrooms, sliced

2 oz. Madeira or sherry wine } add wine along with beans
heat to serving temp.

serves: 4

ZUCCHINI ITALIAN

6 zucchini, sliced
1 onion, cut in rings

} alternate layers of these 2 vegetables in casserole

¼ c. olive oil
4 T. wine vinegar
1 T. honey
1 T. basil
½ t. salt
dash pepper

} combine these 6 ingred.
pour over zucchini
marinate 24 hrs. or longer

serve hot or cold

serves: 6

BEANS BENGAL

1½ lbs. green beans

} blanch beans in boiling salted water 5 min.
drain

2 T. margarine
3 T. good chutney
1½ T. lemon juice
2 T. toasted almonds

} combine these 4 ingred.
toss with beans

serves: 4

NUTTY BEANS

1½ lbs. green beans   } blanch beans in boiling salted water 5 min.
                         drain

1 T. margarine
¼ c. peanuts
¼ c. chopped green onions   combine these 6 ingred. in pan
½ c. sliced mushrooms   saute 6 min.
½ t. seasoned salt   add beans
¼ t. salt   heat to serving temp.

serves: 4

TIPSY BROCCOLI

1 bunch broccoli

} cut into flowerets
  peel stems

3 T. olive oil
1 clove garlic, mashed
1 onion, chopped

} combine these 3 ingred. in pan
  saute 5 min.
  add broccoli

1 c. vermouth (dry)

} add vermouth
  cook covered 5 min.

serves: 4

ITALIAN CHESTNUTS & BRUSSELS

2 pints Brussels sprouts } blanch in boiling salted water 4 min.
drain

1 lb. Italian chestnuts, peeled } layer chestnuts in casserole with brussels

1 c. water
2 vegetable bouillon cubes
salt to taste
½ t. rosemary
½ t. caraway seeds, crushed
} combine these 5 ingred.
pour over brussels
bake covered 350° ½ hr.

serves: 4

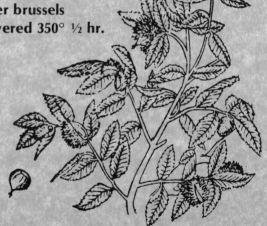

GREEN BEANS FLAIR

2 lbs. green beans

} blanch beans in boiling salted water 5 min. drain

1 can tomato paste
1 T. worcestershire sauce
2 T. mustard
½ t. horseradish
½ t. salt

} stir in these 5 ingred. with beans

serves: 4-6

DELUXE ONION GLAZE

2 lbs. onions, peel, cut in halves
2 T. olive oil
½ t. salt

} quickly saute onions on all sides

¼ c. Madeira wine
¼ c. salad vinegar
3 T. honey
¾ c. chopped dried apricots
grinding pepper

} add these 5 ingred.
cover
simmer 40 min.
uncover
simmer to thicken glaze
pour glaze over onions to serve

parsley

} garnish with parsley

IRISH SPRING CAULIFLOWER

1 head cauliflower

} separate cauliflower
cook 5 min.
drain

1 can condensed cream of
    asparagus soup
½ to ¾ t. curry pd.

} combine these 2 ingred.
heat to serving temp.
pour over cauliflower

serves: 4-6

CHOUX ROUGE

1 head red cabbage, shredded
2 T. margarine   **combine these 5 ingred. in pan**
1 clove garlic, mashed   **cover**
¾ t. salt   **cook 5 min.**
grinding pepper

¼ c. raisins
1 t. sugar   **add these 3 ingred.**
1½ T. vinegar   **simmer 5 min.**

¾ c. sour cream   **stir in sour cream**

                                  serves: 4

Large Red Dutch Pickling Cabbage.

3 T. margarine
½ head cabbage, shredded
½ t. salt

} combine these 3 ingred. in fry pan
saute 6 min.

2 c. cooked noodles

} stir in noodles

6 eggs
¼ c. milk
½ t. salt

} combine these 3 ingred.
beat with fork
pour over cabbage mixture
cook covered gently until almost set

½ c. grated cheddar cheese

} sprinkle cheese over top
cover
turn off heat
let set 1 min.

serves: 4-6

SIMPLE GOURMET DISH

1 cauliflower
¼ t. salt
½ c. water

} cook in boiling salted water 5 min.
drain
puree coarsely

½ c. grated cheddar cheese
½ c. chopped walnuts

} stir in these 2 ingred.
pour into greased casserole
bake 350° 15 min.

serves: 4-6

1 c. raisins
1 c. apricot or orange flavored
    liqueur
} combine these 2 ingred.
marinate several hrs.

¼ t. cinnamon
2 T. lemon juice
½ t. nutmeg
¼ t. cayenne
} add these 4 ingred.
simmer for 1 min.
let stand to cool 5 min.

1 c. mayonnaise
} stir in mayonnaise

1 bunch broccoli, cooked
} serve sauce warm or cold over broccoli

makes 2 c. sauce

CRITTER FRITTERS

2 c. cranberries
½ c. water

} combine these 2 ingred.
cook until just soft

puree

½ c. sugar
1 T. soft margarine
1 t. grated orange rind
½ t. salt
dash allspice
1 c. cracker meal
¼ c. chopped walnuts

} add these 7 ingred.
mix well to make dough

deep fat 360°

} drop by t. into oil

turn when golden
drain on absorbent paper

serves: 6

HI PROTENE ROAST

1½ c. cooked carrots, minced
1½ c. cooked soy beans
1 onion, minced
1 c. whole wheat bread crumbs
½ c. cooked beets, minced
2 T. vegetable oil
2 T. margarine
1 c. water
2 eggs
1 pkg. dried mushroom soup
½ t. sage
1 T. salt

combine all ingred. very well
put into loaf pan
bake 350° 45 min.

serves: 8

Soy Bean

NUT BROWN ROAST

1 c. walnuts, ground
2 c. bread crumbs
2 c. milk
1 onion, grated
2 eggs
1 t. sage
1 t. salt

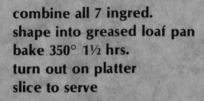

combine all 7 ingred.
shape into greased loaf pan
bake 350° 1½ hrs.
turn out on platter
slice to serve

serves: 4

¼ lb. Edam cheese, grated
1 c. chopped walnuts
1½ c. soft bread crumbs
1 c. milk
1 egg
¼ t. paprika

} combine these 6 ingred.

1 T. vegetable oil
1 onion, minced
1 clove garlic, mashed
½ t. salt

} saute these 4 ingred.
add to mixture
shape in greased loaf pan

bake 375° 45 min.

serves: 4

GRAPE-NUT ROAST DIVINE

1½ c. grape-nuts
1½ c. milk
½ c. cottage cheese
2 eggs
¾ c. nuts, ground
3 t. grated onion
2 T. soft margarine
1 t. celery salt
1 t. salt

combine all 9 ingred. well
shape in greased loaf pan
bake 350° 45 min.

serves: 6

It's great sliced cold in sandwiches

ECONOMY "HAMBURGERS"

2 eggs, beaten
½ c. walnuts, ground
1 c. uncooked oatmeal
3 T. milk
1 T. instant minced onion
1 t. sage
¾ t. salt

combine these 7 ingred.
form into patties

2 T. vegetable oil

brown patties on both sides in oil

½ c. water

add water
cover
simmer until liquid is almost evaporated

makes 8 patties

4 T. chopped onion
2 T. vegetable oil
} saute onion 5 min.

2 eggs, beaten
½ t. sage
2 c. milk
4 c. diced toasted wheat bread
1 c. walnuts, chopped
2 c. cooked lentils, mashed
1 t. salt
}
add these 7 ingred.
mix well
shape into greased loaf pan or casserole
bake 350° 45 min.

apple or cranberry sauce } serve with sauce

serves: 6

~LENTIL

QUICKIE ROAST

2 eggs, beaten
1½ c. milk
1 T. soft margarine
¾ c. nuts, chopped
2 c. bread crumbs
1 c. chopped celery
1 c. cottage cheese
¾ t. sage
1 t. salt

combine these 9 ingred.
let stand 20 min. or more
bake 350° ½ hr.

serves: 4-6

MEAT-NO-MORE ROAST

1 c. cottage cheese
1 c. bread crumbs
¼ c. chopped nuts
2 T. instant minced onions
1 T. vegetable oil
1 T. soft margarine
½ t. poultry seasoning
¼ t. seasoned salt

combine these 8 ingred.
put in loaf pan
bake 350° 20 min.
browned on top

serves: 6

GOURMET "MEAT BALLS"

1 c. walnuts
1 clove garlic
1 onion
1 T. celery
2 T. parsley

} grind these 5 ingred.

½ t. salt
dash pepper
1 c. bread crumbs
2 eggs

} add these 4 ingred.
mix well
shape into balls

3 T. vegetable oil

} saute balls until browned on all sides

1 can tomato sauce
1 can tomato paste
½ c. catsup
1 c. water
2 T. instant minced onion
2 T. instant minced green pepper
1 bay leaf
dash garlic salt
dash celery salt
salt to taste

} combine these 10 ingred.
add meat balls
simmer 1½ hrs.
serve with spaghetti or rice

ITALIAN BAKE

2 eggs
1 onion, minced
1 clove garlic, minced
2/3 c. grated cheese
4 slices whole wheat bread crumbs
¼ c. wheat germ
2 T. milk
½ c. chopped walnuts
¾ t. salt

combine these 9 ingred.
mix well
shape into small balls

3 T. vegetable oil

saute in oil to brown
transfer to baking dish

1 can tomato soup

pour soup over top
bake 325° 20 min.

serve with spaghetti

serves: 6

VEGETARIAN FISH BALLS

¼ c. chopped walnuts
1 c. corn meal mush
1 c. mashed potatoes   } combine these 6 ingred.
1 egg   form into balls
1½ t. salt
½ t. mace

1 egg, beaten   } dip into egg

1 c. dry bread crumbs   } roll in crumbs

½ c. vegetable oil, heated } fry on all sides in oil

tartar sauce   } serve with sauce

serves: 6

MOCK SALMON PLATE

2 c. grated carrots
3 hard-cooked eggs, chopped
½ c. bread crumbs
1 c. minced celery
3 T. grated onion
1 T. lemon juice
¼ c. mayonnaise
¼ c. sour cream
½ t. salt
¼ t. dill weed
dash white pepper

combine these 11 ingred.
mound on 6 beds of lettuce

lemon slices

garnish with lemon

serves: 6

DELUXE "TURKEY" DRUMSTICKS

¾ c. minced onion
1 T. sage
2 T. margarine

} saute these 3 ingred. 6 min.

¾ c. mashed potatoes
1 c. boiled rice
1 hard-cooked egg, chopped
¼ c. chopped mushrooms
¾ t. salt

} add these 5 ingred.
mix well

long spaghetti

} mold mixture into shape of drumsticks
around 4 sticks of spaghetti which
represent the bone

2/3 c. bread crumbs
1 egg beaten

} roll drumsticks in crumbs and egg to coat

¾ c. vegetable oil

} saute drumsticks until browned on all sides

serves: 4-6

SAVORY TUNA BAKE

1 onion, chopped
1 green pepper, chopped
2 T. vegetable oil

} combine these 3 ingred. saute 5 min.

1 can cond. tomato soup
2 T. sugar
3 T. lemon juice
2 t. soy sauce
1 t. salt

} add these 5 ingred. simmer 5 min.

1 7-oz. can tuna, drain
1 sm. can mushrooms

} add these 2 ingred. transfer to baking dish

1½ c. flour
2 t. baking pd.
½ t. salt
¼ c. vegetable oil

} combine these 4 ingred. cut into fine crumbs

(continued next page)

1 egg, separate } put all but 1 t. yolk into ½ c. measure

milk } add milk to egg to equal ½ c.
stir into dough

knead dough on floured surface 10 times
roll ½" thick
cut into ½" wide strips
lay on top of casserole in lattice fashion

1 t. water } add water to reserved 1 t. yolk
brush over dough

¼ c. sesame seeds } sprinkle sesame seeds over top

bake 400° 20 min.

serves: 4

ORIENTAL TUNA CASSEROLE

5 oz. oriental style noodles or
   egg noodles

} cook noodles as pkg. directs
drain
put in casserole

7 oz. can tuna, drained
1 can water chestnuts, sliced

} add these 2 ingred.

1 can cond. cheddar cheese soup
1/3 can milk

} combine these 2 ingred.
pour ½ over casserole

1 can french style green beans,
   drained

} place beans in casserole
top with remaining sauce
bake 350° 40 min.

¼ c. chopped peanuts

} sprinkle nuts over top

serves: 4

1 can cond. cream of mushroom
  soup
1 can mushrooms, drained
2 T. instant minced onion
7 oz. can tuna, drained
¼ c. black olives, chopped
¼ c. stuffed green olives, chopped
2 T. minced parsley
2 c. cooked rice
milk if too dry

combine all ingred.
bake 350° 25 min.

serves: 6

CONFETTI BAKE

7 oz. can tuna, drained
½ t. salt
1 can green beans, drained
1½ c. corn
2 green onions, chopped

} layer these 5 ingred. in casserole

½ c. cornflakes

} top with flakes

bake 350° 20 min.

3 slices cheese

} top with cheese
bake 300° 10 min.

serves: 4

3 ripe avocados } leave unpeeled
cut into halves lengthwise
pit

7 oz. can tuna, drained
¼ t. salt
¾ c. chopped celery } combine these 5 ingred.
1 T. chopped chives spoon into avocado
¼ c. mayonnaise

1/3 c. crushed potato chips } sprinkle over avocados

arrange in shallow baking dish
add ½" water in bottom of dish
bake 400° 15 min.

serves: 6

TUNA-CHEESE STRATA

8 slices bread } arrange 4 slices in 8" square cake pan

4 slices cheese
14 oz. tuna, drained } layer these 2 ingred. on top
top with remaining bread

4 eggs, beaten
2 c. milk
1 t. instant minced onion
dash cayenne
½ t. salt } combine these 5 ingred.
pour over all
let stand 10 min. or more
bake 350° 45 min.

serve hot and puffed

serves: 6

CAULI-SHRIMP PLATE

1 whole cauliflower

} cook cauliflower in boiling salted water 6 min. drain

3 T. margarine
¼ c. chopped green onion
¼ c. minced celery
¼ to ½ t. curry pd.
½ t. salt
dash pepper

} combine these 6 ingred. saute 5 min.

2 T. instant flour

} stir in flour

1½ c. milk

} grad. stir in milk & cook until thickened

1 sm. tomato, diced
1 can sm. deveined cocktail shrimp, drained

} stir in these 2 ingred. heat

cooked rice

} place rice on serving dish
top with cauliflower
pour shrimp sauce over top

VEGETABLE AUX FINES HERBES

2 T. vegetable oil
¾ c. sliced mushrooms
1 onion, chopped
½ green pepper, chopped
1½ t. salt

combine these 5 ingred.
saute 5 min.

½ tumeric
1½ t. Fines Herbes
¼ t. pepper
1 T. minced parsley
2 c. tomatoes, peeled & chopped
1 c. corn
1 c. green peas
¾ c. cooked ABC spaghetti

add these 8 ingred.
transfer to 2 qt. casserole
cover
bake 375° ½ hr.

serves: 4

FLAVOR MELANGE CASSEROLE

2 c. cooked spaghetti } layer spaghetti in bottom of casserole

1 c. sliced carrots
½ c. sliced celery
½ c. mushrooms
½ onion, chopped
½ green pepper, chopped
2 T. vegetable oil

combine these 6 ingred.
saute 8 min.

1 c. corn
¾ T. salt
dash pepper
1 c. stewed tomatoes

add these 4 ingred.
pour over spaghetti

¼ c. corn flake crumbs
¼ c. Parmesan cheese

top casserole with these 2 ingred.
cover
bake 375° ½ hr.
uncover
bake 350° 15 min.

serves: 6

VEGE-RICE CASSEROLE

2 onions, quartered
½ c. rice (wild and white mixed)
½ pkg. dried mushroom soup
2 c. water
½ t. celery salt
1 t. salt

} combine these 6 ingred. in casserole
bake covered 350° 35 min.

1 c. peas
1 c. corn

} stir in these 2 ingred.

1/3 c. grated cheese

} top with cheese
bake uncovered 350° 8 min.

serves: 6

VEGE-RONI

1 c. fine macaroni } cook as pkg. directs
drain

2 T. margarine
1 onion, chopped } saute onion 5 min.

2 c. tomato sauce } add sauce
simmer 5 min.

1/3 c. diced carrots
1/3 c. diced celery
¼ t. poultry seasoning
¾ t. salt
dash pepper } add these 5 ingred.
transfer to baking dish

¼ c. corn flake crumbs } top with crumbs

bake 350° 45 min.

ALL-IN-ONE MEAL

1 cauliflower, separate
3 carrots, sliced
1 pkg. frozen green beans

combine these 3 ingred.
cook 5 min. in small amount water
drain

1 c. corn
1 can stewed tomatoes
6 oz. mushrooms, drained
1½ t. instant minced onion
1 T. instant minced bell pepper
1 T. parsley
½ t. rosemary
1 t. salt

add these 8 ingred.
transfer to casserole
cover
bake 350° 40 min.

serves: 6-8

4 oz. egg noodles, cooked
1 pkg. frozen chopped spinach,
   thawed
¼ c. minced onion
1 T. flour   combine all ingred. in casserole
1 t. salt   cover
dash pepper   bake 350° ½ hr.
¼ c. milk
1 pint cottage cheese
1 T. lemon juice
1 c. sharp cheddar cheese

½ c. crushed potato chips   sprinkle these 2 ingred. over top
3 T. grated cheese   bake uncovered 10 min.

                           serves: 4-6

"Eat your spinach!"

TRIO CASSEROLE

4 potatoes, shredded (2½ cups)
2 onions, chopped
4 lg. tomatoes, sliced
½ c. Parmesan cheese
½ c. grated cheddar cheese
1 t. salt
¼ t. white pepper

} layer these 7 ingred. in baking dish

2 T. margarine

} dot margarine on top

bake 375° 40 min.

serves: 6

BUSY DAY DINNER

1 lb. zucchini, sliced
1 stalk celery, chopped
1 onion, chopped
1 small bell pepper, chopped
2 T. margarine
2 T. olive oil
1 t. salt
dash pepper

combine these 8 ingred. in fry pan
saute 5 min.
transfer to casserole

4 eggs
¼ c. milk
¼ t. salt
dash worcestershire sauce

combine these 4 ingred. in bowl
beat with fork
pour over casserole

¼ c. Parmesan cheese
paprika

sprinkle cheese and paprika over top
bake 400° 15 min. - until set

serves: 4

COMBO EN CASSEROLE

¼ c. margarine
1 onion, chopped
1½ c. sliced summer squash
2 c. sliced broccoli
dash allspice
1 t. salt
dash pepper

} combine these 7 ingred. in fry pan
saute 6 min.
transfer to casserole

1 egg, beaten
¼ c. milk
¼ t. dry mustard
1 t. salt
dash tabasco sauce
½ c. grated sharp cheese
2 T. Parmesan cheese

} combine these 7 ingred.
pour over casserole

¼ c. Parmesan cheese
3 T. bread crumbs
¼ t. seasoned salt

} combine these 3 ingred.
top casserole
bake 375° 20 min. - until custard is firm
serves: 6

BROCCOLI E PASTA

3 T. vegetable oil
1 onion, chopped
1 clove garlic, mashed

} combine these 3 ingred.
saute 5 min.

1 T. margarine
1½ T. instant flour
2 c. milk

} add margarine to pan
blend in flour
grad. stir in milk
cook until thickened

¼ c. Parmesan cheese

} stir in cheese

1 bunch broccoli

} cut broccoli   peel stems
blanch in boiling salted water 5 min.   drain
add to sauce

6 oz. pasta

} cook pasta as pkg. directs   drain
add to broccoli mixture

dash nutmeg, salt & pepper

} season to taste

tomato wedges

} garnish with tomato   serves: 4

BROCCOLI MAIN DISH

1½ lbs. broccoli

} peel stems of broccoli
blanch in boiling salted water 5 min.
drain
lay in buttered baking dish

2 eggs
1 c. cottage cheese
¼ minced green onion
¼ c. grated cheddar cheese
dash tabasco sauce
½ t. salt
dash pepper

} combine these 7 ingred.
pour over broccoli

2 T. melted margarine
1/3 c. bread crumbs

} combine these 2 ingred.
top casserole

bake 350° 25 min.

serves: 4

BROCCOLI CORN BLEND

2 c. chopped cooked broccoli
1 lb. can cream-style corn
½ c. cracker crumbs
1 egg, beaten   } combine these 7 ingred. in casserole
1 T. instant minced onion
½ t. salt
dash pepper

¼ c. cracker crumbs   } sprinkle over top
2 T. Parmesan cheese   bake 350° 45 min.

serves: 6

BRUSSELS ROULADE

8 T. margarine
1 c. chopped green onion
} saute onion 1 min.

1 c. instant Pillsbury's flour
1 t. salt
4 c. milk
} add flour and salt to pan
blend well
grad. stir in milk   cook until thickened
* reserve ½ of white sauce for later use

4 egg whites
4 egg yolks
} beat whites stiff
beat yolks lightly
slowly stir yolks into hot sauce
fold in whites

(continued next page)
} grease 15x10x1" jelly roll pan
line with wax paper
grease and flour paper
spread mixture evenly in pan
bake 325° 45 min.

1 box Brussels sprouts } shred brussels finely   discarding cores
cook in sm. amt. water 3 min.
drain well
mix in with 1/3 of reserved white sauce
spread brussels over baked eggs

1 c. shredded cheddar cheese } sprinkle ½ cheese over

gently peel off paper while rolling up in jelly roll
fashion - using knife if necessary
top with remaining sauce and cheese
bake 350° 5 min.

to serve: cut into thick slices

serves: 6

TANGY BRUSSELS

2 lbs. Brussels sprouts } blanch in boiling salted water 5 min.
drain
place in casserole

1½ c. chopped celery
½ green pepper, chopped } saute these 3 ingred. 5 min.
1 T. margarine

1½ c. cheese sauce
1 t. prepared horseradish } add these 5 ingred.
½ t. worcestershire sauce heat
¼ t. salt pour over brussels
dash pepper

½ c. bread crumbs } sprinkle crumbs over top

bake 400° 25 min.

serves: 4

CREAMY CAULIFLOWER BAKE

1 cauliflower, separated

} cook cauliflower 5 min.
drain
lay in casserole

1 env. spaghetti seasoning mix
¼ c. fine dry bread crumbs

} combine 1 T. seasoning with crumbs

½ c. sour cream
¼ c. mayonnaise
2 T. milk

} combine these 3 ingred. with remaining spaghetti seasoning
pour over cauliflower

top with seasoned crumbs

1 T. margarine

} dot top with margarine

bake 350° 25 min.

serves: 4-6

CAULIFLOWER SCALLOP

3 lg. potatoes, sliced   } parboil vegetables 4 min.
1 cauliflower, broken in pieces   drain

¼ lb. grated cheddar cheese
¼ c. margarine   } layer these 4 ingred. in casserole with
3 T. instant flour   vegetables
1 t. salt

milk   } add milk to reach top of vegetables

bake at 350° 1 hr.

serves: 6

ARMADILLO

1 lg. eggplant } slice ¾ way through eggplant sidewise at ¼" intervals

2 onions, sliced
caraway or other cheese, sliced } place onion and cheese in between slices
lay in casserole

spaghetti or tomato sauce } pour sauce over top

bake 350° 1 hr.

DOUBLE DELIGHT EGGPLANT - protein and flavor!

4 sm. eggplants }
cut into halves lengthwise
scoop out centers and chop pulp
place shells in shallow baking dish

¼ c. chopped onions
1 T. vegetable oil
½ c. rice }
saute onions 4 min.
add rice & fry 3 min.

¾ c. water
¾ t. salt
3 drops tabasco sauce }
add these 3 ingred.
cover
cook 10 min.
add chopped eggplant
cook 10 min.   adding water if necessary

1 egg
¾ c. cottage cheese
1 T. parsley }
stir in these 3 ingred.
stuff eggplant shells
cover with foil
bake 350° 45 min.

8 strips cheddar cheese }
top each eggplant with cheese
return to oven to melt

serves: 4-6

BUSY DAY EGGPLANT DISH

1 lg. eggplant
¼ c. boiling salted water

} cook eggplant 5 min.
drain
layer in bottom of casserole

1 can cond. mushroom soup
1½ c. cooked rice
1 can water chestnuts, sliced
¼ c. chopped green pepper
2 tomatoes, cubed

} combine these 5 ingred.
pour over eggplant

½ c. Parmesan cheese

} sprinkle top with cheese
bake 350° ½ hr.

serves: 4-6

EGGPLANT TOKYO STYLE

1 lg. eggplant

} peel eggplant
slice ½" thick
quarter slices

1½ c. chopped green onion
½ c. soy sauce
1/3 c. lemon juice
½ c. dry sherry
¼ c. chili sauce

} combine these 5 ingred.
alternate with eggplant in casserole
cover
bake 350° ½ hr.

serves: 4

EGGPLANT SAUCE

prepare eggplant as in previous recipe, however:

bake covered 325° 1½ hrs.

puree mixture

**serve this salty, tangy sauce over
vegetables or use as a dip for raw
vegetables**

EGGPLANT CUSTARD CASSEROLE

2 slices bread, cubed
1 med. eggplant, sliced
¼ t. salt
1 c. pot cheese or ricotta
½ t. Italian herbs
¼ t. salt
2 lg. tomatoes, sliced
¼ t. salt
½ c. chopped green onions
½ c. shredded cheddar cheese

layer these 10 ingred. in casserole in the order given

2 eggs
1 c. milk
¼ t. salt

combine these 3 ingred. well
pour over casserole
bake 350° 40 min.

serves: 6

MUSHROOM LAYER ULTIMA

5 slices dark bread } line 9" square cake pan with bread

1 lb. fresh mushrooms, sliced
6 slices cheddar cheese } layer these 3 ingred. on bread
¼ c. sliced black olives

8 oz. tomato sauce
½ t. basil
¼ t. rosemary } combine these 4 ingred. spread over top
½ t. salt

1½ T. flour
½ t. salt
½ c. milk } beat together these 4 ingred. pour over casserole cover with foil
1 egg

bake 350° ½ hr.

serves: 4

COTTAGE POTATOES DELUXE

2 c. hot mashed potatoes
2 c. cottage cheese
½ c. sour cream
2 T. instant minced onion
1 t. salt
dash white pepper

combine these 6 ingred.
pile into greased casserole

1 T. milk
margarine
paprika

brush top with milk
dot with margarine
sprinkle paprika over

bake: 450° 15 min.
       350° 10 min.
(top should be delicately browned)

serves: 4

2 pkgs. frozen chopped spinach } thaw & drain spinach

¾ c. sour cream
½ t. horseradish } combine these 5 ingred.
½ t. prepared mustard fold into spinach
¼ t. salt put into greased casserole
dash pepper

6 hard-cooked eggs } cut eggs in halves lengthwise
mash yolks

2 T. minced onions } mix these 5 ingred. into yolks
¼ t. prepared mustard stuff into whites
¼ t. salt place eggs on top spinach
dash white pepper cover
3 T. mayonnaise bake 375° 15 min.

serves: 6

SQUASH WHIP

1 pkg. frozen squash, thawed
1 onion, minced
12 Ritz crackers, crumbled
2 eggs, beaten
½ c. milk
2 drops tabasco sauce
½ t. salt
dash pepper

} combine these 8 ingred. in casserole

¼ c. Parmesan cheese

} top casserole with parmesan
bake 350° ½ hr.

serves: 4

Hubbard Squash

PATTY PANS

4 patty pan summer squash

> cut off stem ends
> blanch in boiling salted water 4 min.
> drain
> scoop out inside leaving shells whole

salt

> sprinkle salt inside of shells

½ c. croutons
¾ c. crumbled blue cheese

> combine these 2 ingred.
> fill shells

place in shallow baking dish
broil 5 min. to melt cheese

serves: 4

TOMATO EN CROUTE

9" unbaked pie crust ¼ c. mayonnaise	brush mayonnaise over crust bake 450° 5 min.
3 half-green tomatoes	slice tomatoes in shell
¼ t. garlic salt 1½ t. salt dash pepper	sprinkle seasonings over
½ c. mayonnaise 1/3 c. Parmesan cheese 1/3 c. grated Monterey Jack	combine these 3 ingred. spread over top bake 350° 40 min.

serves: 6

6 zucchini

}

simmer zucchini in water 5 min.
drain
cut in ½ lengthwise
scoop out centers
layer in baking dish

1½ c. chopped tomato, drained
2 t. chopped parsley
¾ c. bread crumbs
2 T. melted margarine
½ t. salt
dash pepper

}

combine these 6 ingred.
stuff zucchini

Parmesan cheese

}

sprinkle cheese over tops

bake 350° 15 min.

serves: 6

ARTICHOKES FLORENTINE

1 bunch spinach, cleaned } cook spinach 5 min.
drain
puree

1¾ c. canned hollandaise sauce } mix sauce into puree

4 artichokes } cook artichokes in salted water 40 min.
drain
remove chokes
fill with spinach mixture

parsley } garnish

serves: 4

FORMAL ATTIRE BEANS

1 pkg. frozen beans, thawed
½ c. raisins
3 whole cloves
¼" piece crystalized ginger
½ t. salt
¼ c. water

combine these 6 ingred.
cover
simmer 4 min.
drain
remove cloves

1 c. cooked rice
2 T. peanut butter
salt to taste

add these 3 ingred.
heat to serving temp.

¼ cup pine nuts

toss in nuts to serve

serves: 4

½ c. bouillon
1 t. instant onion
1 T. red wine vinegar
1 t. paprika   combine these 7 ingred.
1 T. cornstarch dissolved in   cook stirring until thickened
1 T. water
dash garlic salt
½ t. salt

1 pkg. frozen string beans,   add beans
   thawed   heat 2 min.

½ c. chopped walnuts   sprinkle nuts over top to serve

     serves: 4

1 bunch broccoli

} peel stems & slice broccoli
blanch in boiling salted water 5 min.
drain
put into serving dish

2 bunches spinach, cleaned
2 T. Madeira or white wine
¼ t. salt

} combine these 3 ingred.
cover
cook 4 min.

puree

4 T. mayonnaise
2 T. Parmesan cheese
¼ t. seasoned salt

} add these 3 ingred. to puree
pour over broccoli

serves: 4

GUACAMOLE BRUSSELS

1 lb. Brussels sprouts

} cut each brussel in ½ through core
blanch in boiling salted water 4 min.
drain

1 bunch spinach, chopped
2 T. water
½ t. salt

} add these 3 ingred. to brussels
cook covered 2 min.

turn off heat
let stand 2 min.
drain well

½ avocado
1 T. lemon juice
1 pkg. guacamole dip mix

} combine these 3 ingred.
toss with vegetables

serves: 4

CAULIFLOWER SUPERB

2 onions, chopped
¾ c. chopped celery

} combine these 6 ingred.
gently saute 20 min.
stirring often

y

} add these 4 ingred.
cover
simmer 7 min.
puree ½ of mixture

} add sour cream to puree

pour puree over remaining cauliflower
heat to serving temp.

serves: 4-6

FROSTED CAULIFLOWER

prepare tomatoes as in Saucy Tomatoes recipe on page 181

1 cauliflower

break cauliflower into flowerets
cook 5 min.
drain
transfer to baking dish
top with tomatoes and sauce

bake 350° 20 min.

serves: 4-6

COLACHE

3 T. margarine
1 clove garlic, mashed
1 onion, chopped
1 green pepper, chopped

combine these 4 ingred.
saute 5 min.

4 zucchini or other summer
   squash, sliced
1 tomato, peeled & chopped
1½ c. corn
1 T. chili pd.
1 t. salt
dash pepper

add these 6 ingred.
cover
simmer 5 min.

serves: 6

CAPONATINA

1 lg. eggplant, 1" slices
¼ c. salt
1 qt. water
} combine these 3 ingred.
let stand 1 hr.
drain well
cut into 1" squares

¼ c. olive oil
} heat oil & saute eggplant on all sides
remove from pan & reserve

2 T. olive oil
2 cloves garlic, mashed
2 onions, chopped
1½ c. celery, chopped
½ t. salt
dash pepper
} add these 6 ingred. to pan
saute 6 min.

2 T. tomato catsup
½ c. water
1 lg. tomato, peeled & chopped
2 T. capers
½ c. sliced ripe olives
} add these 5 ingred.
cook 10 min.

CAPER

(continued next page)

5 T. wine vinegar
1½ T. sugar
salt to taste

} add these 3 ingred.
simmer 5 min.

serve hot or cold

serves: 4

ZUCCHINI O'S

4 zucchini, sliced
2 T. water
¼ t. salt

} cook zucchini in salted water 4 min.
drain

1 can Spaghetti O's

} add spaghetti
heat to serving temp. only

serves: 4

CHINESE VEGETARIAN

½ lb. bean sprouts
½ lb. mushrooms
1 can waterchestnuts, sliced
2 T. vegetable oil

combine these 4 ingred.
saute 5 min.

1 c. peas
1 sm. can fruit cocktail & juice

add these 2 ingred.
heat 1 min.

1 T. arrowroot or cornstarch
3 T. soy sauce
½ t. lemon juice

combine these 3 ingred.
stir to dissolve
stir into vegetables

cook until thickened

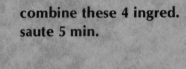

rice
soy sauce

serve with rice & soy sauce

serves: 4

¼ c. margarine
½ c. chopped onions
¼ c. minced celery
¼ c. minced carrots
1 lb. sliced mushrooms

} combine these 5 ingred.
saute 5 min.

2½ c. tomato sauce
2 T. parsley
½ t. oregano
½ t. basil
½ t. marjoram
1 bay leaf
1 t. salt
dash pepper

} add these 8 ingred.
cover
simmer 45 min.
remove bay leaf

spaghetti or noodles

} serve over pasta

Parmesan cheese

} top with cheese

serves: 4

BLACK-EYED PEAS

1 lb. fresh black eyed peas,
   shelled or canned (drain)
1 onion, diced
⅛ t. saffron
1 clove garlic, mashed
1 whole red pepper
¾ t. salt
dash pepper
2 T. vegetable oil

combine these 8 ingred.
saute 7 min.

½ c. rice
¾ c. bouillon

add these 2 ingred.
cook covered 20 min.

imitation bacon bits

sprinkle over top to serve

serves: 4

2 T. margarine
1 onion, chopped
24 almonds

} combine these 3 ingred.
saute 5 min.

1 can bamboo shoots, drained
½ c. mushrooms
2 T. raisins
1 pkg. frozen snow peas and
      water chestnuts, thawed

} add these 4 ingred.
cook 5 min.
stir often

½ c. pineapple juice
1½ T. cornstarch

} combine these 2 ingred.
stir in
cook until thickened

1 c. pineapple chunks

} add pineapple
heat

rice
soy sauce

} serve with rice
and soy sauce

serves: 4-6

Water Chestnut ($\frac{1}{10}$ natural size).

Fruit (natural size).

PICNIC POTATO SALAD

4 c. cooked potatoes
1½ c. chopped celery
½ c. chopped green onions
½ c. chopped pickles
¼ c. sliced radishes
¼ c. ripe olives
2 T. parsley
½ t. celery seed
2 t. prepared mustard
1 T. vinegar
1½ t. salt
dash white pepper
1 c. mayonnaise

combine these 13 ingred.
toss
refrigerate until ready to serve

tomato wedges
hard-boiled eggs

garnish with tomato and eggs

serves: 4-6

ON-TOP-STOVE SCALLOP

2 lg. potatoes, sliced thin
2 onions, chopped
¾ c. milk
2 T. margarine
2 T. worcestershire sauce
1 c. sharp cheddar cheese
1 t. salt
dash pepper

combine all ingred. in fry pan
cover
gently cook until potatoes are tender - ½ hr.

serves: 4

COUCOU - a must!

¾ lb. spinach
1 bunch water cress
2 onions
¼ head lettuce
} mince these 4 ingred.

Water-cress

1 c. raisins
¾ c. chopped parsley
¼ t. curry pd.
¼ t. cinnamon
2 t. salt
dash pepper
7 eggs, beaten
} add these 7 ingred.
let stand 10 min.

2 T. vegetable oil
1 T. margarine
} combine oil and margarine in lg. fry pan
top with spinach mixture
flatten evenly
cook 8 min.
invert by sliding onto plate and returning to pan
cook 5 min.

cut into wedges to serve   serves: 4

4 lg. firm tomatoes	} cut tomatoes into ½" thick slices
½ c. flour pinch basil 1 t. salt dash pepper	} combine these 4 ingred. in paper bag add tomato slices shake to coat
3 T. margarine	} melt margarine in fry pan lay in tomato slices
¼ c. brown sugar	} sprinkle ½ of sugar over top brown carefully turn & sprinkle with remaining sugar
¾ c. milk	} add milk cook until bubbly carefully transfer tomatoes to serving dish cook sauce stirring for a few min. pour over tomatoes

serves: 6

A' JEH - don't miss this!

½ green pepper, minced
½ c. chopped parsley
¼ c. chopped mint
3 green onions, chopped
1 clove garlic, mashed
½ lb. zucchini, grated
1 t. salt
½ t. pepper
3 eggs, beaten
4 T. flour

} **combine all ingred.**

2 T. vegetable oil

} **heat oil in fry pan
drop A'jeh ½ c. at a time in pan forming
pancakes
gently brown on both sides**

serves: 4

EGG PIZZA GRAND TREAT

2 c. biscuit mix
2/3 c. milk

> combine these 2 ingred.
> knead 10 times
> roll into 12" round to fit pizza pan or fit
> baking sheet
> make ½" rim around edges

oil
8 hard-cooked eggs

> brush dough with oil
> slice eggs over dough reserving 6 center
> slices for garnish

salt
pepper

> sprinkle seasoning over

¼ c. chopped onion
¼ c. thyme
¼ t. oregano
½ t. salt

> combine these 4 ingred.
> sprinkle over

2 c. shredded cheddar cheese

> sprinkle cheese over
> bake 450° 20 min.
> crust browned and cheese bubbly
> garnish with egg slices

serves: 4-6

ITALIAN PIZZA

1 pkg. yeast
1¼ c. warm water

} sprinkle yeast over water
let stand 5 min. to dissolve

2 T. vegetable oil
2 c. flour
1 t. salt

} stir in these 3 ingred.

2 c. flour

} work in flour
knead dough 10 min.   until smooth
cover with towel
let dough rise until doubled - 2 hrs.
knead dough down
divide into 4ths rolling each into 9" circles
place on oiled pans turning up edges

oil

} brush dough with oil

(continued next page)

1 c. tomato sauce
½ t. oregano
½ t. basil
1 t. salt
dash pepper

combine these 5 ingred.
spread over dough

sliced mushrooms
chopped onion
minced parsley
chopped green pepper
chopped olives

top with your choice of toppings

Swiss or mozzarella cheese

top with cheese
bake 450° 15 min.

serve brown and crisp & cut into wedges

makes 4 9" pizzas

QUICHE LORRAINE

1 prepared pie shell	} bake 10 min.
¼ lb. grated Swiss cheese	} layer cheese into crust
3 eggs, beaten 1½ c. milk 3 green onions, chopped 1 t. salt dash pepper	} combine these 5 ingred. pour into pie shell bake 370° 45 min. until set but not dry

let stand 15 min.

serves: 4

"NEW LAID EGGS, EIGHT A GROAT—CRACK
'EM AND TRY 'EM!"

HASTY GOLDEN PIE

4 slices bread

} line sides and bottom of buttered 9" pie pan with bread

¾ c. grated carrots
¼ c. sliced black olives
½ c. grated cheddar cheese

} spread these 3 ingred. over bread

2 eggs
1 c. milk
¼ t. salt
dash white pepper

} combine these 4 ingred.
pour into pie
bake 350° 30 min.

serves: 4

SWISS EGG DISH

2 apples, peeled & sliced thin
2 T. margarine

} saute apples 2 min.

2 T. grated Swiss cheese
¼ c. dry vermouth

} add these 2 ingred.
make 2 wells

boiling bouillon ⅛" deep in pan
2 eggs

} break eggs in wells
cook til whites of eggs are set
transfer to serving plates

salt
pepper
paprika

} sprinkle seasonings over top

serves: 2

1 can cond. mushroom soup
1 can sliced mushrooms, drained
¼ c. dry vermouth

} combine these 3 ingred. in pan
heat gently to simmer

4 eggs

} break whole eggs into sauce

salt
pepper
Parmesan cheese

} sprinkle these 3 ingred. over eggs
cover
simmer 4 min. to set whites

fluffy rice

} serve over bed of rice

serves: 4

FONDUE OMELET

1 slice crusty bread
¼ c. stale beer

} soak bread in beer 3 min.

4 eggs
½ t. salt
dash pepper

} beat in these 3 ingred.

2 T. margarine

} heat margarine in fry pan
pour in egg mixture

¼ c. Swiss cheese, diced

} add cheese
cover
cook over low heat until set but not dry
slide onto heated platter

serve while hot
and puffy

serves: 4

6 egg yolks
1 c. cottage cheese
¾ c. light cream or
   evaporated milk
3 T. chopped parsley
¾ t. salt

combine these 5 ingred.
beat to blend well

6 egg whites

beat whites til stiff
fold into yolk mixture

1½ t. margarine

melt margarine in pan
add eggs
cover
gently cook until just set

strawberries or blueberries

if desired, serve topped with fruit

serves: 4

BEAN SPROUT OMELET

3 T. margarine
1 c. chopped green pepper
1 c. sliced green onions
½ lb. bean sprouts
1 can waterchestnuts, sliced

combine these 5 ingred.
saute 5 min.

4 eggs
¼ t. M.S.G.
2 t. soy sauce
1 t. salt
dash pepper

beat together these 5 ingred.
pour over vegetables
cook until just firm
slide onto serving plate

serves: 4

3 T. vegetable oil } heat oil in pan

3 eggs, beaten
1 green pepper, diced
3 stalks celery, diced
1 onion, chopped
1 can mushrooms, drained
1 pkg. frozen chopped spinach,
   thawed & drained

} combine these 6 ingred.
pour into pan
cover
cook 8 min. until golden on bottom
turn to brown other side

1 c. bouillon
1 t. sugar
1 T. soy sauce
¼ c. water

} combine these 4 ingred. to make sauce
heat to boiling

2 t. cornstarch
¼ c. cold water

} combine these 2 ingred.
stir into sauce
cook until thickened

boiled rice } serve egg foo-yung with rice & sauce   serves: 2

APPLE NOODLE PUDDING

8 oz. pkg. noodles } cook noodles as pkg. directs

2 c. cottage cheese
1 c. sour cream
1 c. apple sauce
3 eggs, beaten
1 t. cinnamon
½ t. allspice
2 T. soft margarine
1 t. salt

combine these 8 ingred. with noodles
put into greased baking dish

½ t. cinnamon
½ t. sugar } sprinkle top with these 2 ingred.

bake 350° 1 hr.
then 400° 10 min. (until set but not too dry)

8 oz. noodles

} cook noodles as pkg. directs
drain

¾ t. cinnamon
2 c. cottage cheese
¾ c. sour cream
1 egg

} combine these 4 ingred.
add to noodles
transfer to casserole
cover
bake 350° 35 min.

serves: 4-6

NOODLES ROMANOFF

3 c. cooked noodles
2 c. cottage cheese
1 c. sour cream
½ c. sliced almonds
1 T. instant minced onion   } combine these 9 ingred. in casserole
1 T. instant minced green pepper
¼ c. sliced green olives
1 T. soy sauce
½ t. salt

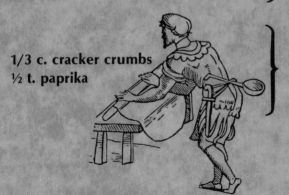

1/3 c. cracker crumbs
½ t. paprika

} sprinkle these 2 ingred. over top
cover
bake 350° ½ hr.
uncover
bake 5 min.

serves: 6

RICH NOODLE DISH

1 pkg. spinach noodles

} cook noodles as pkg. directs
drain

1 c. mushrooms, sliced
1 onion, chopped
1 clove garlic, mashed
1 T. vegetable oil

} combine these 4 ingred.
saute 4 min. in oil

1 c. tomato sauce
24 ripe olives, chopped
¼ lb. grated yellow cheese

} add these 3 ingred.
combine with noodles in casserole

1/3 c. bread crumbs

} top with crumbs
bake 350° 45 min.

serves: 6

NOODLES SUPREME

8 oz. noodles } cook noodles as pkg. directs
drain

1 c. sour cream
½ c. minced onion
1 clove garlic, mashed } add these 6 ingred.
2 T. worcestershire sauce transfer to 2 qt. casserole
dash tabasco sauce
1 t. salt

1 c. shredded Monterey Jack
cheese } top with these 2 ingred.
1 c. bread crumbs bake 350° 35 min.

serves: 6

6-8 oz. large macaroni shells

} cook macaroni as pkg. directs
drain

4 T. margarine
½ c. chopped walnuts
1 t. cinnamon
¼ c. brown sugar

} combine these 4 ingred.
stuff some into shells
toss with remaining mixture
transfer to casserole

bake 350° 15 min.

serves: 4-6

Sugar Cane

GARNISHED MACARONI & CHEESE

8 oz. elbow macaroni, cooked
2 c. grated yellow cheese
1/3 c. milk
½ c. sliced stuffed olives
¼ c. sliced green onions

} combine these 5 ingred. in casserole

6 tomato slices

} top with tomato

½ c. bread crumbs
¾ t. seasoned salt

} sprinkle these 2 ingred. over top

1 t. margarine

} dot top with margarine

bake 350° 20 min.

serves: 4

2½ oz. instant potato flakes } cook as pkg. directs

2 eggs, beaten
1 t. salt
about 1½ c. flour
} add these 3 ingred. to make smooth dough
roll out ½" thick
cut 3" squares

10-12 plums } peel and pit plums

1 t. cinnamon
½ c. sugar
} combine these 2 ingred.
fill plums
put 1 plum in each dough square
fold to enclose plum and make ball

boiling salted water } cook dumplings in water 10 min.
drain

1 c. bread crumbs
¼ c. margarine
} combine these 2 ingred. in pan
saute to toast crumbs lightly
roll dumplings in crumbs
bake 350° 10 min.

serves: 6

CHEESE POLENTA

1 c. yellow cornmeal
3½ c. boiling water

} very slowly add cornmeal to water
stirring constantly

2 T. instant minced onion
½ t. salt
3 T. margarine
1 egg, beaten
¾ c. Parmesan cheese

} stir in these 5 ingred.
pour into 9x9" baking dish

¼ c. Parmesan cheese

} sprinkle cheese over top

put under broiler 4 min.

serves: 6

PANCAKE BAKE

¼ c. margarine } melt margarine in lg. fry pan

½ c. flour
½ c. milk
2 eggs, beaten
dash allspice

} combine these 4 ingred.
mix only to blend
scrape into buttered pan
bake 350° 15 min.

1 pkg. frozen creamed spinach } cook spinach as pkg. directs
use as filling for pancakes

serves: 2-4

APPLE PANCAKE SUPREME

1 c. flour
¼ c. sugar
dash salt
2/3 c. milk
} combine these 4 ingred. to make creamy batter
let stand ½ hr.
thin with more milk if necessary

3 T. margarine } melt margarine in fry pan

1 delicious apple, peeled } thinly slice apple into pan
saute 4 min.
pour batter over apples
cover
shake pan over med. heat to brown bottom
of cake (about 9 min. - top will be firm)

2 T. sugar } sprinkle sugar on top of pancake

place plate on top of pan
invert together so that cake is transferred to plate

(continued next page)

1 T. margarine } melt margarine in pan
flip pancake back in pan to brown other side
shake over heat 5 min.

2 T. sugar } sprinkle sugar over pancake

bake 450° 3 min.

2 T. sugar
1 t. cinnamon } sprinkle these 2 ingred. on serving platter
invert pancake on platter

sour cream
strawberries or other fruit } garnish with sour cream and fruit

¼ c. brandy } heat brandy
ignite
pour flaming over pancake

serves: 4 with dreams of more

PANCAKE ROULADE

favorite pancake mix	} prepare as pkg. directs
cottage cheese	} place 2 T. cheese on each pancake
strawberries	} layer strawberries over cheese
	roll up pancakes to enclose filling
strawberry flavored syrup or apple sauce	} top with syrup or sauce

POOR KNIGHTS

3 egg yolks
2 c. milk
1 T. sugar
dash salt

} beat together these 4 ingred.

12 stale bread slices

} soak bread in mixture until saturated

3 egg whites, lightly beaten
2 T. water
1 T. sugar

} combine these 3 ingred.
dip bread into mixture

fine bread crumbs

} dredge in crumbs

1 T. margarine

} slowly saute in margarine until puffed and brown

syrup or apple sauce

} serve with syrup or sauce

serves: 6

BUDGET DINNER

2 stalks celery, chopped
¼ c. chopped green onion
1 T. vegetable oil
} saute these 3 ingred. 4 min.

6 eggs
¼ t. salt
¼ c. milk
} beat together with fork these 3 ingred.
add to pan
cover
gently cook until almost set

4 slices cheddar cheese
} top with cheese

1 lb. cooked broccoli
½ c. milk
1 T. (instant Pillsbury) flour
} combine these 3 ingred.
puree
heat 2 min.
pour over eggs

serves: 4

PINEAPPLE BOATS

1 ripe pineapple with top

} quarter pineapple lengthwise cutting through core

cut out pineapple in chunks leaving shell
and core intact to form boats

½ c. Kirsch liqueur

} add Kirsch to chunks
marinate several hrs.

return chunks to shell

serves: 4

RUMMY BANANAS

4 firm bananas, peel ¼ c. rum	} marinate bananas in rum 1 hr. turn occassionally
1 egg, slightly beaten	} dip bananas in egg
½ c. cooky crumbs	} roll bananas in crumbs
¼ c. margarine	} melt margarine in fry pan
	fry bananas on all sides until browned
whipped cream	} may serve with whipped cream serves: 4

PEAR BLUSH

2 firm pears	} peel cut in half core pears
1 c. water ¾ c. sugar 1 T. lemon juice 2 sticks cinnamon	} combine these 4 ingred. bring to boil add pears simmer uncovered 8 min. turning once
	let cool in syrup remove pears to serving plate
¾ c. cottage cheese	} beat cheese smooth fill pears
marachino cherry	} top with cherry
¼ c. chopped walnuts	} sprinkle over
	serves: 4

APPLES SCANDINAVIA

4 lg. apples, peel and halve 2 c. water 2 T. lemon juice ¼ c. sugar	combine these 4 ingred. simmer 7 min. remove apples with slotted spoon place single layer cut side down in buttered 10 inch pie pan
¼ lb. margarine 2/3 c. sugar	cream together these 2 ingred.
3 egg yolks	beat yolks one at a time
½ c. ground almonds 2 t. grated lemon rind	beat in these 2 ingred.
3 egg whites	beat whites stiff and fold into batter

lightly spread batter over apples
bake at 350° for 20 min.

serve at room temp.

LEMON SHERBET WITH BLUEBERRY SAUCE

¾ c. lemon juice
2/3 c. sugar
1 T. grated lemon peel
dash salt
2 c. condensed milk

combine these 5 ingred.
pour into ice cube tray
freeze until outer edges are solid
pour into bowl
beat until smooth

return to tray
cover with foil
freeze until firm

2 pkgs. frozen blueberries

thaw and drain berries reserving juice

1 T. cornstarch

dissolve cornstarch in juice
cook until thickened
add berries
cook 1 min.
cool to room temp.
serve over sherbet

serves: 4-6

STRAWBERRY YOGHURT COOKIES

2¼ c. flour
¼ t. salt
1 t. baking pd.
¼ c. vegetable oil
1 egg
1/3 c. sugar
½ c. strawberry yoghurt
¼ c. strawberry jam

combine all ingred.
mix well
roll out ¼" thick
cut in circles
place on greased cooky sheet
bake 350° for 13-15 min.

SESAME COOKIES

1 c. toasted sesame seeds
½ c. coconut
2 c. flour
1 t. baking pd.
½ t. soda
½ t. salt

}   combine these 6 ingred.

¾ c. soft margarine
½ c. brown sugar
1 egg
1 t. vanilla

}   combine these 4 ingred.
cream smooth
blend into dry ingred.
shape into walnut size balls

place on cooky sheet
flatten with fork tines
bake 350° 12 min.

PEANUT-RAISIN COOKIES

1 c. flour
½ t. baking pd.
¾ t. baking soda
¼ t. salt

} **combine these 4 ingred.**

½ c. vegetable oil
½ c. peanut butter
1/3 c. sugar
½ c. brown sugar
1 egg

} **combine these 5 ingred.**
blend with dry ingred.

1 c. raisin bran cereal

} **mix in cereal**

shape 1 inch balls on cooky sheet
flatten with fork tines
bake 375° 10 min.
let stand on sheet 1 min.

makes 4½ dozen cookies

DEEP DISH APPLE COBBLER

4-5 delicious apples } slice to fill ¾ casserole

1 t. cinnamon
juice of ½ orange } sprinkle these 2 ingred. over

1 c. yoghurt
½ c. sugar
1¾ c. flour
1 t. baking pd.
¼ t. salt } combine these 5 ingred.
spread evenly to cover apples

2 T. sesame seeds } sprinkle seeds over top

bake 325° 1 hr.

ECONOMY APPLE PIE

2 c. boiling water
1 c. sugar
¾ stick margarine
2¼ t. cream of tartar
pinch nutmeg

} combine these 5 ingred. in pan
bring to boil

30 Ritz crackers

} drop crackers into mixture
boil 2 min.

1 9-10" unbaked pie shell
1½ T. cinnamon

} sprinkle cinnamon in pie shell
fill with cracker mixture
bake 450° 15 min.

ice cream

} serve with ice cream

STRAWBERRY CHEESE PIE

1 envelope unflavored gelatin
¼ c. cold water

} sprinkle gelatin over water to dissolve
let stand 5 min.
bring to boil
reserve

1 c. cottage cheese
8 oz. cream cheese, soften
¼ c. milk
½ c. sugar
1 T. lemon juice
dash salt

} combine these 6 ingred.
blend smooth
beat in gelatin

9 inch baked pastry shell

} fill shell

2 c. strawberries

lightly press strawberries into top

chill 2 hrs.

serves: 6

SOUR CREAM LUSCIOUS LEMON

1 baked 9" graham cracker crust

1 c. sugar
3 T. cornstarch
¼ c. margarine
1 T. grated lemon rind
¼ c. lemon juice
3 egg yolks

} blend together these 6 ingred. in pan

1 c. milk

} stir in milk
cook stirring constantly until thick
cool

¾ c. sour cream

} fold in sour cream
spoon into pie shell

chill to serve

serves: 6-8

1 lb. can pitted cherries, drain
4 c. sliced apples
½ c. sugar
2 t. cinnamon
½ t. nutmeg
dash salt

} toss together these 6 ingred.

1 unbaked 10" pie shell

} fill pie shell

2 T. margarine

} dot margarine over top

½ c. brown sugar
1/3 c. flour
½ c. cornmeal
½ c. soft margarine

} combine these 4 ingred.
mix with fork until crumbly
spread over pie
bake 350° 1 hr.

whipped cream or
cheddar cheese

} serve with ice cream or cheese

BANANA BAKE

dough for 2 crust pie ⎫ pat ¾ dough into bottom and sides of baking dish
⎭ reserve ¼ of dough

3-4 apples, peel
2 bananas
1 t. cinnamon ⎫ toss together these 6 ingred.
¼ c. sugar ⎬ fill baking dish
1 t. orange peel ⎭ crumble reserved dough over top
3 T. orange juice

1 T. sugar ⎫ sprinkle these 2 ingred. over top
dash cinnamon ⎭ bake 350° 35 min.

½ c. ground almonds
½ c. wheat germ
1 c. flour
½ c. sugar
½ c. soft margarine
yolks of 2 boiled eggs
½ t. lemon peel
dash cinnamon
dash salt
3 t. almond extract

combine these 10 ingred.
cut together with a fork
chill dough 2 hrs.
roll out ¾ dough to fit sides and bottom
of spring form pan.

1 c. raspberry jam

spread jam over top

roll out remaining dough
cut into ½ inch wide strips
top in lattice fashion
bake 350° ½ hr.

RICE IMPERIAL

1 c. rice

} cover rice in cold water
bring to boil
simmer 5 min.
drain

2½ c. milk
6 T. sugar
½ t. salt

} add these 3 ingred.
cover
cook 15 min.
turn off heat
let stand 10 min.

1½ t. vanilla
2 bananas, diced
1 c. chopped walnuts
¾ c. crushed pineapple, drain

} toss in these 4 ingred.

ice cream
whipped cream

} serve warm with either

serves: 6-8

Budget-minded shoppers are facing a duo challenge in the marketplace today. They must not only keep a sharper eye out for bargain buys on surpluses and slow moving items, but they must be on guard against price gimmicks. These gimmicks include: confusing isle displays where "featured" and "special" does not mean a mark down in price; the shrinking package; short weights, counts and measures; a lessening of quality control; and saturation advertising designed to lure you into unnecessary purchases.

Price-fighting consumers can counterattack by patronizing only those markets that are consistently making an effort to bring you quality foods at sensible prices and by refusing to purchase any item that is being excessively inflated in price or deflated in quality. In this period of accelerating food prices, it is absolutely essential for thrifty homemakers to realize learning how to budget and shop is as important as learning how to cook.

On the next two pages are six suggestions for coping with the supermarket crisis and trimming the family food budget.

1. Meal planning time is the time to put your money-saving, calorie-sparing and cholesterol-lowering ideas to work. A big step in this direction is to replace many meat-rich meals with inexpensive, nutritious and flavorful meatless meals. With the great enthusiasm being generated for meatless meals it has now become acceptable, if not fashionable and adventurous, to serve meatless meals to your family and guests. To add additional savings to already lower costs, plan exciting and imaginative meatless meals around the less expensive, in-season and plentiful fruits and vegetables and incorporate dairy products as a rich source of low-cost complete protein. You can further economize by preparing hearty main course soups and by cutting waste by using perishables and leftovers without delay.

2. With 100 million or more Americans fighting off excess pounds, budget-watchers must realize the price paid for weighing too much. A person 20 pounds overweight requires 300 extra calories per day just to maintain the added fat. If it costs 50 cents a day to furnish these 300 calories you are adding $15 a month, and nearly $200 a year, to your grocery bill. Plugging this dollar drain becomes crucial when several overweights are eating from the same food budget. Serving low-cost, low-calorie meatless meals and serving smaller portions of all foods at all meals, will help both weight reduction and cost reduction.

3. A well-planned shopping list is indespensible in safeguarding against over or careless buying. The list should be based on advertised food specials, menu plans and the re-stocking of basic food items. By heading your shopping list with the Basic Four Plus One Food Groups (see Nutritional Guidelines pages 7&8) you are forced to think nutritionally and satisfy your basic nutritional needs before purchasing other foods. And by placing the expensive and high cholesterol meat group last, you will stress the more economical, yet highly nutritious, protein alternatives. To have a complete shopping list, you should keep a running list and make a quick check of the refrigerator and storage areas before shopping.

"Do you use a shopping list?"

4. **Be an informed shopper.** Read the labels and keep track of prices. If a rapid jump in price is spotted, be flexible enough to seek a less expensive substitute or a new item, even if it means revising menu plans or changing your shopping list. Determine your best buy by comparing different brands and different sizes of the same brand and by determining and comparing the expected cost-per-serving from various items. While bargain hunting, smart shoppers must watch for price gimmicks. Also be on the lookout for unadvertised sales and unexpected low priced items that can find a place in your eating plans.

5. It has been estimated grocery costs can be cut nearly in half by eliminating the urge to splurge. The impulse purchase represents one of the biggest threats to conserving your health food dollars. Snack foods and drinks, high priced convenience items, and fun and party foods all fall into this category. To help avoid these budget-busting buys, it is wise to shop alone, take your time, and be leery of slick packaging, heaping isle displays, and fancy names. And above all, don't shop when hungry, for the hungry shopper is more apt to overindulge.

6. Be especially alert at checkout time for your savings may be lost. Knowing prices will help you check the checker. Have items selling together placed together to avoid an item being totaled at a higher individual price. Also, guard against items being totaled twice, make sure the scale registers zero, and count your change. Remember, the area surrounding the checkout counter is loaded with impulse items designed to inveigle you into more purchases. Also remember, having to wait in line offers you one last chance to change your mind on an impulse buy. Don't be reluctant to request an item be deleted from your purchases. Make it a point to leave without the "checkout counter blues" and go home a supermarket winner.

✳ One last reminder, the sharp shopper can easily achieve a savings of up to 15% or more by careful shopping. Attempting to save makes sense, since staying within the budget does let everyone enjoy their food more.

"Does the scale register zero?"

BOOKS FOR READING AND REFERENCE

THE FAMILY GUIDE TO BETTER FOOD AND BETTER HEALTH. Deutsch, R., Creative Home Library, 1971. Paperback edition, Bantam Books, Inc.

NUTRITION AGAINST DISEASE. Williams, R. J., Pitman Publishing Corporation, 1971. Paperback edition, Bantam Books, Inc.

THE TRUTH ABOUT WEIGHT CONTROL. Solomon, N., Stein and Day Publishers, 1972. Paperback edition, Dell Publishing Co., Inc.

DIET FOR A SMALL PLANET. Lappe, F.M., paperback, 1971, Ballantine Books, Inc.

NUTRITIVE VALUE OF FOODS. U.S. Department of Agriculture. Home and Garden Bulletin No. 72. A comprehensive table of nutritive values for household measures of commonly used foods. Available from: Superintendent of Documents, Government Printing Office, Washington, D.C. 20402. Cost: 85 cents.

A large number of other excellent, and inexpensive, government publications in the areas of budget and finance, food, diet and nutrition, and health are also available from the Government Printing Office in Washington, D.C. For more information, request a copy of the current Consumer Infomation Index or visit one of the eighteen Government Printing Office Bookstores located in major cities around the country.

THE RECIPE INDEX

For the cook's convenience, the recipes are listed by the name of recipe,
name of vegetable, and category of recipe (appetizer, soup, etc.).

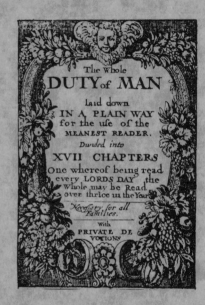

The Whole
DUTY of MAN
Laid down
IN A PLAIN WAY
for the use of the
MEANEST READER.
Divided into
XVII CHAPTERS
One whereof being read
every LORDS DAY the
whole may be Read
over thrice in the Year
Necessary, for all
Families.
With
PRIVATE DE
VOTIONS

240

If you should put this rare collection of delectable, nutritious and money-saving recipes to frequent use, you may find your family and friends falling in love with the cook. But please, share the conviviality by recommending this cookbook to others.

If additional copies of this, or the companion budget-minded, health conscious book **The Meat Stretcher Meal Guide** (216 pages, illustrated and indexed), are unavailable at your bookstore, send check or money order in the amount of $4.50 per book to The Ryan Company. Postage and handling included. Please add sales tax if delivered in California.

THE RYAN COMPANY

2188 Latimer Lane   Los Angeles, Ca. 90024